Music and Mourning

While grief is suffered in all cultures, it is expressed differently all over the world in accordance with local customs and beliefs. Music has been associated with the healing of grief for many centuries, with Homer prescribing music as an antidote to sorrow as early as the 7th Century BC. The changing role of music in expressions of grief and mourning throughout history and in different cultures reflects the changing attitudes of society towards life and death itself. This volume investigates the role of music in mourning rituals across time and culture, discussing the subject from the multiple perspectives of music history, music psychology, ethnomusicology and music therapy.

Jane W. Davidson is a singer and stage director with research interests in performance and expression, voice, musical development and wellbeing. She was Editor of *Psychology of Music* (1997–2001), Vice-President of the European Society for the Cognitive Sciences of Music (2003–2006) and President of the Musicological Society of Australia (2010–2011). She is currently Professor of Creative and Performing Arts (Music) at The University of Melbourne and Deputy Director of the Australian Research Council Centre of Excellence for the History of Emotions. She has published over 100 scholarly contributions and secured a range of grants and awards in both Australia and overseas.

Sandra Garrido is a pianist, violinist and researcher in music psychology. She completed her PhD at the University of New South Wales and subsequently spent several years in post-doctoral research at the Melbourne Conservatorium of Music and the Australian Research Council Centre of Excellence for the History of Emotions, exploring the use of music in depression in both the modern day and historically. She is currently a National Health and Medical Research Council and Australian Research Council Dementia Research Fellow at the MARCS Institute for Brain, Behaviour and Development at Western Sydney University. She has published over 30 academic publications including a book co-authored with Jane Davidson entitled *My Life As A Playlist* (2014).

Music and Change:
Ecological Perspectives

Series Editors:

Gary Ansdell, Nordoff Robbins and University of Exeter, UK
Professor Tia DeNora, Department of Sociology & Philosophy, HuSS,
University of Exeter, UK

Series Advisory Board:

Kenneth Aigen, Temple University, USA
Jane Davidson, University of Melbourne
Timothy Dowd, Emory University, USA
Lucy Green, Institute of Education, UK
Lee Higgins, Boston University College of Fine Arts, USA
Raymond MacDonald, Edinburgh University, UK
Mercédès Pavlicevic, Nordoff Robbins, UK
Even Ruud, University of Oslo, Norway
Brynjulf Stige, University of Bergen, Norway
Henry Stobart, Royal Holloway, University of London, UK

Music and Change: Ecological Perspectives, is a cross-disciplinary, topic-led series for scholars and practitioners. Its aim is to explore the question of how, where and when music makes a difference. If music is a dynamic ingredient of change, what are the processes and mechanisms associated with music's powers, and how can ecological perspectives help us to understand music in action? Book proposals are welcome in any of the following areas: healthcare, social policy, political activism, psychiatry, embodiment, mind and consciousness, community relations, education and informal learning, management and organizational cultures, trauma, memory and commemoration, theories of action, self-help, conflict and conflict resolution, the life course, spirituality and religion, disability studies, palliative care, social criticism, governance, resistance, protest, and utopian communities.

Published titles in the series

The Passion for Music: A Sociology of Mediation
Antoine Hennion, translated by Margaret Rigaud and Peter Collier

Musical Pathways in Recovery
Gary Ansdell and Tia DeNora

Music and Mourning

Edited by

Jane W. Davidson and Sandra Garrido

LONDON AND NEW YORK

First published 2016
by Routledge
2 Park Square, Milton Park, Abingdon, Oxon OX14 4RN

and by Routledge
711 Third Avenue, New York, NY 10017

Routledge is an imprint of the Taylor & Francis Group, an informa business

© 2016 selection and editorial matter, Jane W. Davidson and Sandra Garrido; individual chapters, the contributors

The right of Jane W. Davidson and Sandra Garrido to be identified as the authors of the editorial material, and of the authors for their individual chapters, has been asserted in accordance with sections 77 and 78 of the Copyright, Designs and Patents Act 1988.

All rights reserved. No part of this book may be reprinted or reproduced or utilised in any form or by any electronic, mechanical, or other means, now known or hereafter invented, including photocopying and recording, or in any information storage or retrieval system, without permission in writing from the publishers.

Trademark notice: Product or corporate names may be trademarks or registered trademarks, and are used only for identification and explanation without intent to infringe.

British Library Cataloguing in Publication Data
A catalogue record for this book is available from the British Library

Library of Congress Cataloging in Publication Data
Names: Davidson, Jane W. | Garrido, Sandra.
Title: Music and mourning / edited by Jane W. Davidson and
   Sandra Garrido.
Series: Music and change: ecological perspectives | Includes index.
Identifiers: LCCN 2015042125 (print) | LCCN 2015043828 (ebook)
Subjects: LCSH: Funeral music—Psychological aspects. | Bereavement—
   Psychological aspects. | Funeral music—History and criticism.
Classification: LCC ML3830.M815 2016 (print) | LCC ML3830 (ebook) |
   DDC 781.5/88—dc23
LC record available at http://lccn.loc.gov/2015042125

ISBN: 978-1-4724-5879-7 (hbk)
ISBN: 978-1-315-59664-8 (ebk)

Typeset in Times New Roman
by Swales & Willis Ltd, Exeter, Devon, UK

Printed in the United Kingdom
by Henry Ling Limited

Dedicated to the memory of Philippa Maddern
(24 August 1952 – 16 June 2014)

Contents

List of Figures and Examples		ix
List of Tables		x
Notes on Contributors		xi

1 On Music and Mourning **1**
JANE W. DAVIDSON AND SANDRA GARRIDO

2 The Modern Funeral and Music for Celebration: Part I **9**
SANDRA GARRIDO AND JANE W. DAVIDSON

3 The Modern Funeral and Music for Celebration: Part II **18**
SANDRA GARRIDO AND JANE W. DAVIDSON

**4 'The Ceremony of Tolling the Bell at the Time of Death':
Bell-ringing and Mourning in England c.1500–c.1700** **31**
DOLLY MACKINNON

5 Haunting Music: Hearing the Voices of the Dead **40**
HELEN DELL

**6 The Psychological Function of Music in Mourning Rituals:
Examples from Three Continents** **55**
SANDRA GARRIDO AND WALDO F. GARRIDO

**7 'Under the Bruised Sky': Music and Mourning in
Post-revolutionary Iran** **69**
SARAH WALKER

**8 Restoring Songs: On Mourning and an 'Everyday'
Performance Genre in Northern Australia** **83**
SALLY TRELOYN

viii *Contents*

9 Music Therapy and Mourning

KATRINA SKEWES MCFERRAN AND ALEXANDER HEW DALE CROOKE

97

10 Embracing Life in the Face of Death: Community Singing with the Elderly

JANE W. DAVIDSON

114

Index

127

Figures and Examples

3.1	Personal variables and music choices for following tradition motivation	25
3.2	Personal variables and music choices for personal expression motivation	25
3.3	Personal variables and music choices for aesthetic motivation	25
3.4	Personal variables and music choices for mood creation motivation	26
5.1	'The Twa Sisters' (Binnorie), musical transcription, anon., as sung by Custer LaRue	44
5.2	'The Twa Sisters' (Binnorie), text transcription, anon., as sung by Custer LaRue (from CD liner notes)	44–5
5.3	'The Cruel Mother', musical transcription, anon., as sung by Shirley Collins	46
5.4	'The Cruel Mother', text transcription, anon., as sung by Shirley Collins	46–7
7.1	The cover of Helali's *Moharram 1384* VCD (2005)	75
7.2	The cover of Helali's *Moharram 1385* DVD (2006)	76
7.3	Image of Helali on his 2007–2008 website, which also promoted 'Haj Abdorreza Helali' (sic) ringtones	77
7.4	Profile picture for a *Facebook* group dedicated to Helali, 2009	77
7.5	Reza Helali's *Facebook* profile picture, 2009	78
8.1	Buyu: song and gloss by Scotty Nyalgodi Martin, c.1973	91

Tables

2.1	Study 1 participants	13
2.2	Emergent themes from interviews	14
3.1	Survey options for reason for funeral music choice and percentage of participants who selected them in the pilot study	28
3.2	Survey options for reason for funeral music choice and Reason Cluster in the large-scale study	28
10.1	Group participants	117
10.2	Dominant themes from the data	119

Notes on Contributors

Alexander Hew Dale Crooke is a postdoctoral research fellow at the University of Melbourne in the fields of music therapy and social policy. He has an academic background in social science and has worked as a professional researcher on numerous projects spanning the fields of music therapy, social science, psychology, social services, epidemiology, policy development and environmental studies.

Jane W. Davidson has published five books and over 100 other scholarly outputs. Her research is in the area of music performance studies, focusing largely on psychological approaches. She is the current Deputy Director of the Australian Research Council's Centre of Excellence for the History of Emotions and Professor of Creative and Performing Arts (Music) at the University of Melbourne.

Helen Dell is a research fellow in the Department of English and Theatre Studies at the University of Melbourne. Her research is in the fields of medieval music and literature, especially when joined together as song. She has published two books: *Desire by Gender and Genre in Trouvère Song* (Boydell and Brewer, 2008); and *Music and the Medievalism of Nostalgia: Fantasies of Medieval Music in the English-speaking World, 1945 to 2010* (Cambia Press, 2014).

Sandra Garrido has a broad research interest in music psychology and particularly in the relationship between music and mental health. She is a postdoctoral research fellow for the Centre of Excellence for the History of Emotions and the MARCS Institute for Brain, Behaviour and Development at Western Sydney University. She has published in numerous academic journals and has co-written a book with Jane Davidson, *My Life as a Playlist* (UWA Publishing, 2014).

Waldo F. Garrido is Associate Lecturer in Music in the Department of Media, Music, Communication and Cultural Studies at Macquarie University in Sydney. He is also a bassist, composer, singer, re-mixer and producer working with various pop, Latin and jazz bands. His research interests include cultural memory and nostalgia, music performance and production (digital technologies), and world popular music (cross-cultural music making).

xii *Notes on Contributors*

Dolly MacKinnon is Associate Professor at the University of Queensland in Brisbane. Her research and publications span history and music, analysing the mental, physical and auditory landscapes of past cultures. Her latest book is *Earls Colne's Early Modern Landscapes* (Ashgate, 2014).

Katrina Skewes McFerran is Professor of Music Therapy and Co-Director of the National Music Therapy Research Unit at the University of Melbourne. She has researched and published about the value of music with young people in a range of contexts. Her latest book is *Creating Music Cultures in Schools: A Perspective from Community Music Therapy* (Barcelona Publishers, 2014).

Sally Treloyn works on the song and dance traditions in the Kimberley region of northwest Australia, and on developing strategies to support Indigenous stakeholders and organizations in their efforts to sustain their highly endangered musical practices. She is a postdoctoral research fellow at the University of Melbourne and Coordinator of the National Recording Project for Indigenous Performance in Australia.

Sarah Walker is a postdoctoral fellow, researching Iranian cultural history and based in Australia.

1   On Music and Mourning

Jane W. Davidson and Sandra Garrido

This book investigates the role of music in mourning rituals across time and culture. As an inter-disciplinary volume, cultural history, ethnomusicology, psychology and music therapy form the basis of the studies presented.

Regulation of emotion is clearly important, and music can provide a powerful tool for the 're-ritualization' of grief and a re-discovery of personal expressions of grief. Rituals are an important part of the grieving process and these have been extensively documented by cultural anthropologists (Reeves & Boersma, 1989–1990). According to archaeologist Brian Hayden (1987), rituals have been performed by humans for over 100,000 years. Music often has an important role to play within such rituals of mourning (Schechter, 1994).

Music has been associated with the 'healing' of grief for many centuries, with Homer recommending music as an antidote to sorrow around the seventh or eighth century BC (Nelson and Weathers, 1998). Recent studies have also shown the benefits of music-therapy in dealing with grief (Dalton & Krout, 2005; Hilliard, 2001; McFerran, Roberts, & O'Grady, 2010). The anthropological literature reveals that in many cultures specialised music within the funeral ritual allows the externalisation of feelings and a social medium in which grief can be acceptably expressed (Castle & Philips, 2003; Goss & Klass, 1997).

Regionally, specific religious traditions have been strongly associated with rituals of mourning, particularly funerals. The music used in such rituals would, in the past, also have been based primarily on local religious customs. However, more recent decades have seen the secularisation of funerals and a stripping away of traditional religious practices in many parts of the world (Emke, 2002). Scholars note that grief rituals are not as available for use in American culture as they were prior to the twentieth century (Klass, Silverman & Nickman, 1996). Similarly, in Australia after the First World War a deep cultural shift occurred lasting until the 1980s in which thoughts and feelings about death were often avoided, rituals and expressions of grief were minimised and sorrow became a private matter (Jalland, 2006). This deterioration in the role of traditional rituals has often led to insufficient grieving and inadequate grief resolution (Romanoff & Terenzio, 1998).

A second major shift in cultural responses and attitudes to death and grief has occurred since then in many parts of the world (Jalland, 2006). This has been stimulated by globalisation as waves of migration have encouraged diversity

2 Jane W. Davidson and Sandra Garrido

in attitudes and approaches to grief. Psychologists have also contributed to the change, by encouraging the view that open emotional expressions of grief can be healing. Kubler-Ross (1969) for example, popularised theories about 'stages' of grieving and emphasised the individuality of people's responses to grief.

Despite the increased secularisation of funerals, rituals are therefore progressively becoming a part of the grieving process once again. New rituals, often spontaneously created, have emerged that reflect modern perspectives on grief and mourning even when conducted in traditional contexts such as churches (Cook & Walter, 2005). This is illustrated by the widely broadcast funeral of Princess Diana at Westminster Abbey in 1997 in which tradition was accompanied by the spontaneous expression of grief by thousands of people around the world and by personal tributes from those who were close to her (Garces-Foley & Holcomb, 2005). These new and more personal manifestations of grief often focus on celebrating the life of the deceased even more than they do on loss and death.

Music has a large role to play in this re-ritualisation of mourning. Music played at contemporary funerals may be pieces of special significance to the deceased rather than traditional music for funeral services (Wouters, 2002). As Saynor (2001) puts it: 'many are discovering new music, new words and new rituals that are helping them express their spirituality' (p. 22). Even where music choices may seem bizarre or even irreverent to some attendees, these personalised expressions allow the bereaved to celebrate and memorialise the life of the deceased in a very individual way.

Thus, contemporary music choices for funerals have become life interpreting, reflecting important changes in cultural approaches to questions of life and death. Beyond the funeral, therapists are making use of music to help mourners create other forms of rituals for coping with their loss. Castle and Philips (2003) thus express the hope that these new rituals will enable many to 'make room in their lives for a relationship with grief, to learn and grow from that relationship' (p. 62). The function of music within modern-day grief rituals is thus an important area warranting further investigation in future research.

The chapters included in this volume look at such questions as how music is used to modify our thoughts and feelings about loss in various cultural settings, how this was done in the past, current trends, and future projections. The authors consider the use of music in a variety of ceremonial and formal contexts as well as more family-oriented and personal contexts that surround mourning. The discussions include historical investigations that explore the use and function of music for mourning across different periods and places. The volume also includes work drawing out the relevance of music to mourning in contemporary Western societies such as Australia and considers some experimental approaches based on psychology research paradigms.

The chapters deal first with music used in formal contexts such as funerals and second with music used in dealing with grief in settings outside the funeral. In Chapters 2 and 3, the results of three empirical studies by Sandra Garrido and Jane Davidson are explored that investigate contemporary choices for funeral music

On Music and Mourning 3

and the motivations behind such choices. Results are discussed in the light of current trends in mourning practices in Western cultures. In Chapter 2, a brief review of the literature relating to historical and current funeral music choices in Western countries is provided. The chapter also reports the results of an explorative study in which five participants were interviewed about the music they would choose for their funeral and the motivations for such choices. Results indicate that music choices reflect a desire to express personal meaning and to celebrate life rather than to focus on loss, and that a tension may at times exist between the desire for personal expression and the need to adhere to religious standards.

In the third chapter, the results of two cross-sectional surveys tested funeral music choices in a student group and a broader sample from the general population. The findings of this study suggest that music choices are related to personality differences including coping style. It is argued that the contemplation and selection of music can therefore form a helpful part of the grieving process of the bereaved or of those contemplating a future death.

In the fourth and fifth chapters, deeper historical perspectives are offered, looking back to practices in Medieval and Early Modern Europe. In Chapter 4, Dolly McKinnon looks at the role of bells tolling in seventeenth-century Christian death rituals in England. Bells were in fact used to announce the cycles of life and death, regulate the seasons, and also, through sounds or silences, articulate the religious and political adherences of individual parish communities across the English countryside. In rural and urban settings all those who lived within earshot of church bell towers knew the particular sounds of their parish bells. McKinnon reflects on this practice as an example of an emotional community of practice. Through case studies, she demonstrates how bell sounds for the dead could both unite and divide parish communities as form part of their rituals of death, burial and mourning.

In the fifth chapter, Helen Dell deals with a very different kind of practice: the revenant ballads of the Medieval British Isles, which reveal to their singers and audiences the voices of the dead as imagined by the ballad writer. Sometimes the message seems simply to communicate that the loved one is dead, in a distant place; sometimes the mourner is encouraged to stop mourning and get on with life; sometimes the ghost comes back to pronounce judgement or exact revenge. These imagined voices of the dead speak with surprising authority, appearing to know more than the living and sometimes wish, or are compelled, to return and impart their knowledge. Through investigating the words the living place in the mouths of the dead in these songs, this chapter reflects on what these words tell us of ourselves and how we mourn. It adopts the theoretical lens of psychodynamics, a theoretical framework that developed from Freud's work at the beginning of the twentieth century, to make meaning of these far-distant historical practices.

In Chapter 6, Sandra Garrido and Waldo Garrido engage with cultural contexts other than those of Western European origin, considering three examples of the use of music in funerals from three different continents: the jazz funeral of various regions in the United States, the lament in Georgia and the 'cantos de ángeles' of

4   *Jane W. Davidson and Sandra Garrido*

Chile. They argue that the acts of selecting and/or performing music in mourning rituals are 'task-based' coping activities that both facilitate the expression of grief and create a sense of enduring connection with the deceased. These psychological functions are discussed both in traditional contexts and in contemporary rituals of personalised mourning.

In Chapter 7, Sarah Walker discusses the longstanding tradition of Iranian 'elegiac singing' and its transformation during the recent turbulent history of Iran, as well as examining aspects of the emotional, spiritual and social lives of participants in this form of melodic mourning. Pursing this anthropological investigation, an eighth chapter by Sally Treloyn explores the complex experiences of Australian Aboriginal communities as they face some of the highest rates of death by preventable causes across generations in the world. Grief and loss are also felt in the wake of the forced removal of Aboriginal children from their families in Australia from the 1880s to the 1960s, as well as high rates of attrition of linguistic and musical knowledges. The chapter seeks to better understand these experiences.

In Chapter 9, Katrina Skewes McFerran and Alexander Crooke present an example of how music therapy can play a supportive role in the mourning experiences of adolescents. It includes a review of existing literature regarding how music is used from a therapeutic perspective in contexts of mourning and follows with an illustrative example of a music therapy programme being used to assist secondary school students in dealing with experiences of loss and grief. Extracts of student interviews articulate the value of music in this process from their point of view.

The book closes with the tenth chapter by Jane Davidson who explores 'predeath grief', or 'anticipatory grief' – the feelings of loss associated with death before its occurrence, common among caregivers of the terminally ill or aged. She also engages with the ill or aged themselves who are living in expectation of their own future death and may experience 'preparatory' grief as they cope with the dying process. She explores the way that music can play a vital role in both coming to terms with impending death, and in celebrating life. Singing in particular can provide both joy and a sense of companionship for those dealing with grief prior to the loss of their own lives or that of a loved one. This chapter examines the impact of six community singing groups involving the elderly, patients with dementia, and their carers. Motivations for musical engagement and the effect of the groups on the health and wellbeing of participants are discussed. Results indicate that many participants benefit from the chance to embrace new experiences and meet new companions, as well as the spiritual comfort that singing affords in the face of their fast approaching deaths.

Having summarised the chapters, it is important to us as the writers and editors of this volume to explain to readers the very specific context for this work. It emerged from a panel discussion at a conference on the power of music that included amongst its participants the medieval historian and founding Director of the Australian Research Council's Centre of Excellence for the History of Emotions, Philippa Maddern. The panel took place around the time of Philippa's diagnosis with a fatal illness that sadly resulted in her death shortly before the completion of this volume. The book is dedicated to Philippa's memory, and as such we feel it appropriate to explore the ways music was used in the public rituals undertaken shortly after her death.

Following traditional Christian religious structures, her closest friends and family conceived both the funeral in Perth and a memorial service in Melbourne as events that offered remembrance and honour for Philippa's life, but also proposed emotional comfort and a framework for the congregations present to mourn her loss. Philippa (Pip to her friends and family) was a brilliant person who was a highly successful researcher, teacher and mentor, administrator, loyal and devoted family member and friend, and animal lover who had a deep highly personal Christian structure to her life and who enjoyed science fiction writing and cooking, and was a passionate musician.

Pip's Music

Pip was a great lover of music. She played piano and owned a collection of professional quality recorders that she and her two sisters used to play together. She was a late starter on violin, beginning lessons about five years before she died. She also owned a couple of Balinese flutes and a didgeridoo. She possessed recordings of the medieval music ensemble *Tre fontane* that she played with in Melbourne, as well as many musical souvenirs including CDs and sheet music, especially that from her extensive experience as a choral singer: music folders from college choirs enjoyed during her own student days in Melbourne and in Oxford, as well as parts from a vocal quartet, Sneak's Noise, she had formed in Perth, Western Australia. Pip also used to arrange and compose music: choral writing and music for voice and recorder.

For Pip's funeral and subsequent memorial service, close friends and family decided to choose music that was appropriate to the shape of the funeral liturgy but primarily that Pip had sung and loved and which also aimed to honour fond memories for those who knew and treasured her. There was therefore much care and affection behind the selection. We were fortunate enough to ask Matthew, the person mainly responsible for the music selection, to explain the context for each piece, and his comments help us to unravel the symbolism of each work: the music choices are suffused with remembrances and resonances. Each piece is now described and contextualised to show how the music was able to offer a structure through which memory and grief could be managed.

The Funeral

Choral Settings

Never Weather-beaten Sail (Thomas Campion, 1567–1620)

This part song was suggested by Pip's niece, and was offered as the opening musical item owing to the words 'O come quickly, sweetest lord, and take my soul to rest'. Pip loved it, and had performed it on a memorable holiday with family and friends and a small scratch choir of ex-members of her University Choir.

6 *Jane W. Davidson and Sandra Garrido*

Si bona suscepimus (Orlande de Lassus, 1532–1594)

This was something that Matthew, a very close younger friend, particularly wanted to have sung for Pip. He reported that Pip loved the piece – and the last time he had heard it was when he and his family had sung it with her after Christmas, just months before her death. He reflects on the piece:

> There is, I seem to recall, a modal ambiguity at the conclusion of the piece, which I think provides a ray of hope, as do the wonderful returning settings of *sit nomen domini benedictus*. But it also acknowledges the bleakness of grief and the inexplicability of death. On one occasion, when we sang the motet around the time of her mother's death, Pip said that she wanted it sung at her funeral. It calls for two deep alto voices, which absolutely suited Pip's voice, and also her taste for thick textures.

O sacrum convivium (Thomas Tallis, 1505–1585)

This was a choral part again with two alto lines that Pip, friends and family sang in many different contexts. Matthew regarded it as a beautiful communion anthem, appropriate for a requiem mass. It was yet another piece that was sung with friends at the party and so the connotations of conviviality and feasting was also something that also seemed right for Pip's funeral.

Psalm

Psalm 121 *I will lift up mine eyes* (Henry Walford Davies, 1869–1941)

This is a setting in Anglican chant well known within the Anglican college chapel tradition. This was one work that Matthew chose for its wonderful words rather than Pip's personal fondness for it. On the evening of Pip's death, around her hospital bed, Matthew, his mother, wife and later his brother, read Vespers and Compline from the Benedictine Breviary. After these readings, some psalms were read, lastly this one. This reading/singing of psalms around the death bed is something that appears in St Bede's descriptions of the deaths of early medieval English monks, and was something the friends felt appropriate for Pip with her Christian faith and love of medieval history.

Hymns

The week before Pip died, she sang hymns from her hospital bed (the Vaughan Williams setting of *Come down O love divine* and *Come holy Ghost our Souls inspire*). The day before she died, she roused herself to sing a verse of the hymn *Holy, Holy, Holy* in honour of Trinity Sunday.

The first hymn in the funeral, *I know that my redeemer lives*, was chosen because of the desire to stress the hope of resurrection at the heart of the funeral liturgy. It was also one of her sister's favourite hymns, and comes strongly from the Anglican tradition within which Pip was raised. The second hymn, *Deck thyself my soul with gladness* (Schmücke dich), was a hymn that Pip had really taken to heart during her mother's illness and after her death. She always asked for it to be sung in hymn singing sessions. So it was the obvious choice for a communion hymn at the funeral, and had the added advantage of being a German hymn as Pip loved singing German chorales. The final hymn, *The day thou Gavest, Lord, is ended*, was a family favourite. It was sung at Pip's mother's funeral.

Organ Music

Pip loved the music of J.S. Bach. The introit was his setting of the chorale *O Mensch bewein dein Sünde groß* – sin, the root of death within the Christian narrative, is what is confessed in the opening of the requiem rite. Matthew made a unilateral choice to ask for the Passacaglia in C Minor because he felt that its solemnity, beauty and complexity mirrored both Pip's personality and the unfolding of history.

The Memorial Service

Choral Settings

Thou knowest Lord (Henry Purcell, 1659–1695)
From the famous funeral sentences, Pip sang this work many times. It was found at the front of one of her folders of music at her home. It had also been the introit for the funeral of a dear friend of hers, who had married Pip and her husband at home.

Sicut cervus (Giovanni Pierluigi da Palestrina, c. 1525–1594)
For reflection after the sermon, this was proposed by Pip's niece and Matthew had remembered listening to it with Pip as part of the commencement rite for the Easter Vigil at Westminster Abbey.

Hymns

The opening hymn, *Lord Jesus think on me,* was one that friends sang together with Pip, particularly after her husband's death. Pip was a great descant singer and often sang it in this piece, thus it evoked something of her *joie de vivre*. It was also chosen for its words of comfort. The final hymn, *The Day of Resurrection*, was another German chorale, and was chosen to conclude the service with great hope.

Psalm

The psalm, *The King of Love my shepherd is*, was a favourite hymn of Pip's mother.

Organ Music

A postlude by J. S. Bach was described by Matthew as 'a little serendipity'. It had been suggested by the organist, and Matthew felt is was perfect, mingling virtuosity with joy and sadness.

8 *Jane W. Davidson and Sandra Garrido*

Of course many of us have not experienced anything approaching the musically rich life of Pip Maddern, but we can see how the music for her death rituals was selected with great care and love and that it was used to facilitate understanding, sharing and expressions of grief and loss and remembrance for all present.

Arguably, the study of grief practices takes us to the heart of any culture, illuminating beliefs about the very meaning of existence (Jalland, 2006; Kotthoff, 2001). The vital role that music can play in the lives of those facing death or the loss of a loved one is a noteworthy subject for those seeking insight into the inevitable encounter that all must face with death. The chapters which follow reveal different aspects of music's profound association with mourning.

References

Castle, J., & Philips, W. L. (2003). Grief rituals: Aspects that facilitate adjustment to bereavement. *Journal of Loss and Trauma, 8*, 41–71.

Cook, G., & Walter, T. (2005). Rewritten rites: language and social relations in traditional and contemporary funerals. *Discourse and Society, 16*, 365–391.

Dalton, T. A., & Krout, R. E. (2005). Development of the grief process scale through music therapy songwriting with bereaved adolescents. *The Arts in Psychotherapy, 32*, 131–143.

Emke, I. (2002). Why the sad face? Secularization and the changing function of funerals in Newfoundland. *Mortality, 7*, 269–284.

Garces-Foley, K., & Holcomb, J. S. (2005). Personalizing Tradition. In K. Garces-Foley (Ed.), *Death and Religion in a Changing World*. Armonk, NY: M.E. Sharpe.

Goss, R., & Klass, D. (1997). Tibetan Buddhism and the resolution of grief: The Bardo-Thodol for the dying and the grieving. *Death Studies, 21*, 377–395.

Hayden, B. (1987). Alliances and ritual ecstasy: Human responses to resource stress. *Journal for the Scientific Study of Religion, 26*, 81–91.

Hilliard, R. E. (2001). The effects of music-therapy based bereavement groups on mood and behavior of grieving children: a pilot study. *Journal of Music Therapy, 38*, 291–306.

Jalland, P. (2006). *Changing ways of death in twentieth-century Australia: war, medicine and the funeral business*. Sydney: UNSW Press.

Klass, D., Silverman, P. R., & Nickman, S. L. (1996). *Continuing bonds: new understandings of grief*. Washington, DC: Taylor & Francis.

Kotthoff, H. (2001). Verbal Art Across Cultures: The Aesthetics and Proto-aesthetics of Communication. In H. Knobloch & H. Kotthoff (Eds.), *Aesthetic dimensions of Georgian grief rituals: On the artful display of emotions in lamentation* (pp. 167–194). Tubingen: Gunter Narr Verlag.

Kubler-Ross, E. (1969). *On Death and Dying*. New York: Routledge.

McFerran, K., Roberts, M., & O'Grady, L. (2010). Music therapy with bereaved teenagers: A mixed methods perspective. *Death Studies, 34*, 541–555.

Reeves, N. C., & Boersma, F. J. (1989–1990). The therapeutic use of ritual in maladaptive grieving. *Journal of Death and Dying, 20*, 281–291.

Romanoff, B. D., & Terenzio, M. (1998). Rituals and the grieving process. *Death Studies, 22*, 697–711.

Saynor, J. K. (2001). The new spirituality: issues in bereavement that affect a funeral director's work. *Canadian Funeral News, 29*, 22–23.

Schechter, J. M. (1994). Divergent Perspectives on the Velorio Del Angelito. *Journal of Ritual Studies, 8*, 43–84.

Wouters, C. (2002). The quest for new rituals in dying and mourning: Changes in the we-I balance. *Body and Society, 8*, 1–27.

2   The Modern Funeral and Music for Celebration

Part I

Sandra Garrido and Jane W. Davidson

Introduction

The past two hundred years have seen substantial changes in attitudes towards death in Western Christian cultures. Choices of music for use in funerals can potentially provide an interesting reflection of these changes. Funeral music likely had its origins in ancient chants designed to frighten away spirits (Meyers, Golden & Peterson, 2009). Mention is made of the use of dirges in several funeral scenes in ancient Greek dramas (Whitwell, n.d.). The Romans apparently hired professional mourners to sing songs of praise to the deceased, known as the *Nenia* (Whitwell, n.d.).

In Western cultures Christian music has traditionally dominated funeral services since the inception of the church. In early Christian congregations this would have primarily been the singing of psalms based on Old Testament texts. However, later generations of Christians wrote specific music for use in funerals that differed according to the tradition to which they belonged. In the Catholic tradition, requiems based on the Mass for the Dead were originally chanted by Gregorian monks and later written in polyphonic settings. Later composers such as Mozart, Verdi and Brahms also wrote famous examples of Requiems. In the Protestant tradition Martin Luther, who viewed congregational singing as an important part of worship, wrote a volume of funeral music which was published in 1542 (Leaver, 2002). John Calvin, however, who influenced other branches of Protestantism, discouraged the use of musical instruments during services (although singing was allowed), and limited the number of songs that could be used (Caswell, 2011–2012). Christian music continued to dominate funeral music in Western cultures until the 1970s (Caswell, 2011–2012).

Much of this traditional Christian funeral music was 'solemn' and 'grave' as was believed suitable for the occasion (Gammon, 1988, p. 435). Almost all funeral hymns in seventeenth- and eighteenth-century England, for example, were written in minor keys (Gammon, 1988). Some of the typical funeral songs being used well into the twentieth century included Handel's 'Largo', the hymns 'Abide With Me' and 'The Lord Is My Shepherd', and Chopin's Funeral March (Parsons, 2012), all of which are relatively slow and are often sung or performed quite mournfully.

One author, writing in an Australian newspaper in 1910 describes a volume of funeral marches compiled by Mr E. Crawford which he spent a 'depressing' evening reviewing (TGR, 1910). The volume was said to contain around 60 anthems, some of which were in minor keys and some of which were major. However, the writer states that all of them showed 'more or less evidence of having been composed under stress of sorrow' (p. 20). Numerous works contained therein are described by the author including some by Beethoven and the Funeral March by Chopin, all of them seemingly included in the volume because of their sorrow-evoking capacity. A. E. Floyd (1936) similarly describes the music 'available' for use in memorial services. He groups them into two categories: instrumental and vocal. He goes on to describe the Dead March by Handel, along with the funeral marches of Beethoven and Chopin as being 'at the head' of instrumental music for memorial services for British people. Other music discussed included Guilmant's 'Funeral March and Hymn of Seraphs' for organ, and Sullivan's 'In Memoriam' overture, thus demonstrating the predominance of sorrowful music in music commonly used for funerals at that time.

However, with the rise of cremation and secular funerals in the twentieth century, music choices began to change. As crematoriums became more popular locations for funerals, music became an issue of money. The cost of installing organs for the provision of live music was prohibitive, and so crematoriums began to make use of recorded music, which they called 'relayed music'. That this practice was rare in the 1930s is revealed by the reporting of a demonstration of gramophone-use attended by 300 representatives for cemetery trusts and burial boards in London in the Australian newspaper *The Courier Mail* ('Indian Hawker's Will,' 1933). Mainstream churches also began to consider the need to give funerals a less bleak atmosphere and the use of some famous funeral dirges became less frequent (Parsons, 2012).

A perusal of newspaper archives in Australia during the early decades of the twentieth century reveals some of the differences that were emerging in the way people were using music in funerals at that time. For example, *The News* of Adelaide ('Band At Funeral: Music Lover's Request,' 1924) reports on the funeral of Mr Joseph Weber, a hotel licensee. He is reported to have been a great music lover during his lifetime and specifically requested a band to play at his graveside. The choice of music was 'The Miserere' from Verdi's *Il Trovatore* and the hymn 'Go Bury Thy Sorrow'. The chosen hymn contains lyrics that speak about Jesus lightening the burden of those who are sorrowing, although it is often melancholy in performance. The former choice is certainly a work usually associated with tragedy and 'misery'. The report does not reveal whether Mr Weber himself chose the music or not, but it is likely that these were pieces that were already in the repertoire of the bands involved.

The South Australian *Recorder* ('Indian Hawker's Will: Suitable Music for Funeral', 1933) notes the death of an 'Indian hawker' named Mahango Ram whose will specifically requested the use of 'suitable music' at his funeral and the accompaniment of his funeral procession by two mourning coaches. This latter example provides some interesting insight into the importance of music in

Australian funerals of the time. 'Indian hawkers' were migrants to Australia from India who worked as itinerant hawkers, travelling throughout country regions and selling a diverse range of products, providing an important lifeline for people in rural towns (Jupp, 2002). Mr Ram left an estate worth over 2,000 pounds and specifically requested that news of his death be advertised in both country and city newspapers. Indeed, the same notice was printed in at least two more newspapers, including *The Maitland Daily Mercury* and the *Newcastle Morning Herald and Miners' Advocate.* The Australian Bureau of Statistics reports that a pound in 1901 was equivalent in buying power to about $100 in 2001. In modern terms, therefore, his estate would be worth something in the vicinity of $AUD200, 000. This seems like a significant estate for a travelling salesman at the time who was, presumably, a relatively new resident in the country. The request that his death be widely advertised implies that Mr Ram was well-known and respected. His requests regarding his funeral suggest that it was important to Mr Ram that his funeral be fitting to his status as a respected and well-known member of the community. Likely being of non-Christian background, Mr Ram may not have been personally familiar with what music would be considered appropriate. However, music obviously figured highly in his idea of what a suitable funeral would entail.

Whether the music used in a funeral was mournful or otherwise perhaps depended on the religious tradition to which the deceased belonged, as illustrated by a report of the death of General Bramwell Booth, a Salvation Army missionary in the *Singleton Argus* ('Late Bramwell Booth', 1929). The article states that 'there will be no funeral music; only bright happy songs. The coffin will be borne in triumph in an open touring car' (p. 6). It was not until the liturgical reforms of the 1960s and 70s, however, that a recognisable movement emerged to make mainstream church funerals more personalised and less austere in tone (Parsons, 2012).

In modern settings sacred music may still play a part, but secular music is increasingly involved in funeral services even in church settings (Caswell, 2011–2012; Cook & Walter, 2005). A survey of British funeral music conducted by Co-operative Funeralcare (2013) reveals that bereaved families are increasingly choosing contemporary songs with which they or the deceased personally identify. Amongst the top ten most popular songs they reported in 2012 were 'My Way' by Frank Sinatra and Shirley Bassey, 'Time to Say Goodbye' by Sarah Brightman and Andrea Bocelli, and 'Wind Beneath My Wings' by Bette Midler. They also report some more humorous choices including TV and film music, such as 'Always Look on the Bright Side of Life' by Eric Idle (from *Monty Python's Life of Brian*), and 'It's Time to Face the Music' from *The Muppets.* An Australian funeral services provider reports similar choices and some more unusual ones such as Queen's 'The Show Must Go On' or 'Another One Bites the Dust' (Kelton & Steward, 2008). Thus funeral music has gone from selections primarily dictated by religious custom or church procedure to an 'anything goes' approach where almost anything can be seen as 'appropriate' if it was of personal significance to the deceased.

12   *Sandra Garrido and Jane W. Davidson*

However, the surveys of funeral music mentioned above conducted by commercial entities do not reveal whether the music was chosen by the deceased person themselves or by relatives and family or the funeral organisers. In addition, the motivations for music choices are only able to be speculated upon. Empirical studies of funeral music are, in fact, in surprisingly short supply.

The most comprehensive study to date is that of Adamson and Holloway (2012), which examined the music played at 46 funerals in the UK. The authors reported that the music was important in creating a sense of ceremony and in expressing the spirituality (although not necessarily religiousness) of the bereaved. At the funerals in that study the music appears to have been chosen primarily by the bereaved or the funeral providers themselves, although some participants chose music that would be meaningful to the deceased. However, the authors reported that they were 'rarely able to establish any specific meaning' for the music chosen on the deceased's behalf (p. 46).

Of course the way in which tradition and custom shape rituals often involves complex negotiations among various persons using the options that are available in a given context. Given the variety of choices that are often available for funeral music in both secular and religious settings today, most music chosen at funerals in Western cultures in modern times is likely to reflect personal values, whether such values include religious beliefs or not. There is not necessarily, therefore, a dichotomy between traditional funeral music and music with personal meaning. However, for some people, custom or public perception of appropriateness may be a primary motivating factor. Decisions may therefore be made without conscious thought or decision-making as with several of the participants mentioned by Adamson and Holloway (2012). Furthermore, despite increased freedom of choice, the desire to choose non-religious music may still cause some conflict to occur in religious contexts, with clergy rejecting music that they feel is 'inappropriate' (Parsons, 2012, p. 134).

Thus we conducted a series of studies in which we investigated the extent to which tradition is still important to individuals in making choices for funeral music as opposed to music that is personally meaningful in that it relates to personal memories, values or beliefs. Therefore, the research reported in this chapter and the following chapter ('The Modern Funeral and Music for Celebration: Part II') sought to address the following questions:

1   What kind of music would people in modern times choose to have played at their own funeral or at the funeral of a loved one?
2   What are the primary motivations for such funeral music choices?
3   To what extent is tradition still important to people when making choices about music for funerals in modern times?
4   When traditional music is chosen, to what extent does this reflect personal beliefs, or a desire to follow long-standing cultural or religious customs?
5   What kinds of personality factors may influence the music chosen and the reasons for such choices?

Research Design

This research followed a mixed method research paradigm (Johnson, Onwuegbuzie & Turner, 2007). A sequential exploratory design was used with an initial study involving qualitative analysis of interview data, and a quantitative phase comprised of a pilot study involving a survey of 227 students and a final survey of a broader sample of over 400 participants. The purpose of a sequential exploratory design is to explore a question using the qualitative study and then to use quantitative methods to test elements of a theory which may emerge from the qualitative data (Creswell *et al.*, 2003). In this research, a series of interviews permitted an initial exploration of the research questions. The results were then used in constructing a more comprehensive survey to be used with a broader sample of participants. The rest of this chapter will discuss the results from the qualitative phase, while results of the survey studies are discussed in the following chapter ('The Modern Funeral and Music for Celebration: Part II').

Methods

Participants

Participants were randomly approached at a University campus in Perth, Western Australia, and invited to participate in an interview study. Some of the participants were students and others were academics attending an international conference on the campus. The five participants belonged to age groups ranging from 20 to 50 years of age (see Table 2.1). Of the five, one was male, and two were from non-English speaking backgrounds although the study took place within an English language context.

Data Collection Procedure

After being given a brief description of the project, participants indicated their understanding of the purpose of the project and gave their consent for the data collected to be used for research purposes. They were also asked permission to video the interview.

The interviews were conducted using a general guide approach (Britten, 1995). The interview guide had been developed based upon the research questions and

Table 2.1 Study 1 participants

Participant	Gender	Age Group	Funeral Music Choice
P1	M	30–40	Bach
P2	F	30–40	Classical, but finish with something light-hearted
P3	F	40–50	Joyous music
P4	F	20–30	A 'graduation' song
P5	F	20–30	Instrumental music

14 *Sandra Garrido and Jane W. Davidson*

was designed both to find out how willing participants would be to speak about such a topic, as well as information about their music choices. Participants were asked about their broad music tastes as well as the music they would choose to mark other major life events such as weddings or a twenty-first birthday. In relation to funeral music, participants were firstly asked what music they would like to have played at their funeral, and the interviewer then attempted to draw them out further to discover the motivations for their choice.

Data Analysis

Thematic analysis was used for examination of the narratives collected during the interviews. The interviews were first transcribed as described by Braun and Clarke (2006). Codes were generated from an initial reading of the material, and the data were then systematically allocated to the chosen codes (Miles & Huberman, 1994). The codes under which the data were sorted were: tradition, emotional content, social connection, personal meaning and celebration. Once the data had been sorted according to these codes, the patterns were analysed and combined to create themes and sub-themes (see Table 2.2).

Results

The participants discussed a diverse range of music that they would choose to be played at their funerals (see Table 2.1). Most participants did not name any particular piece of music. However, all participants were able to name a style or a type of music that they thought would create the kind of atmosphere they would prefer. These primarily reflected a desire to have music that held some personal significance for them or that would create the desired mood at the funeral.

Table 2.2 Emergent themes from interviews

Following Tradition	*Create Certain Mood or Emotion*			*Express Personal Meaning*
	Emotional Content	*Social Connection*	*Celebration*	
Music that people know	Emotional	Grieving as one through music that everyone knows	Light-hearted; leave people laughing	Personal taste
Mournful music	Not overly emotional		Joyous music	Music which 'stood out' in life
Appropriate to setting; suitable	Serious for the ceremony		Graduation music – moving on	Reflects own lifestyle
Permitted by church				

Participant 1 (P1) said that he would choose to play Bach despite it being an 'obvious' choice. He described it as being 'emotionally laden, but not too over-the-top' and since it was well known to most people it would enable the mourners to 'grieve as one'. P2 said she would also choose classical music since she was herself a classical musician and this was therefore the kind of music that meant the most to her. She also described classical music as being the genre she considered most suitable to the setting of a funeral. However, she indicated that although she would choose something serious for the ceremony itself, she would prefer to finish with something 'light-hearted' so as to 'leave them laughing at the end'.

The idea of playing music that was cheerful and not too mournful was a recurrent theme with several of the participants. P3 also said she would choose 'joyous music', particularly music that had stood out for her throughout her life, although she expressed concern that this may not be 'allowed' in a church situation. Similarly, P4's choice of 'graduation' music, which would signal that she had merely moved on to a new phase of existence rather than ceased to exist, was based on a desire that people not be 'too devastated'. In contrast, P5, who was of Chinese origin, seemed most concerned with tradition and the appropriateness of the music to the occasion, describing music that should be dignified, preferably instrumental music with no lyrics. This kind of music, she felt, would be most likely to convey the seriousness and respect necessary for the occasion.

Thus, while some participants gave consideration to tradition and 'appropriateness' (P5), the desire to leave mourners in a cheerful frame of mind or to express one's personal values also had a large influence on music choices. In fact, at least one participant seemed torn between following tradition and/or church dictates and being permitted to create the environment that she would desire (P3).

Discussion

Thus, three overall motivations were identified: to follow tradition, to create a certain mood or emotional state, and to express something personal. The participant most concerned with following tradition was of Chinese origin, which is not surprising given the relative importance given to tradition among Chinese people as compared to those of Western origin. Nevertheless, one Christian participant also expressed concern over the possible clash between her desire to express something personal and what might be permitted by her church. This suggests that despite the more individualistic outlook of people in modern Western countries like Australia, tradition and 'appropriateness' are still of concern.

All participants were interested in creating a particular mood with their music choices. Despite nominating classical or serious and 'appropriate' music, all participants except for one expressed a desire to add something humorous, light-hearted or hopeful. The participant who was an exception to this felt that the use of music which was not dignified or serious would be disrespectful to the deceased person. Thus, wanting to minimise grief in mourners or to be remembered with joy and celebration played a large part in the thinking of the participants.

16 *Sandra Garrido and Jane W. Davidson*

Also of importance to participants was to use music that was personally significant, such as music that they had played as performers or music that had been a part of their lives at significant times. This was of greater weight to most participants than the following of tradition. This study further illustrated how the music played at funerals, to some extent, mirrors changing attitudes to death in society at large. Our historical review revealed the predominance of mournful music, whether classical or religious, in funerals of the past in Western cultures. However, with increasing secularisation, funerals tended to become less formal and to focus less on loss and grief. This trend can be seen slowly emerging from funeral music choices in the first half of the twentieth century. Non-empirical surveys, along with the data from the participants in our case studies presented in this chapter, tends to suggest that today, celebration and the minimisation of grief are of more importance than the following of tradition.

However, this study was exploratory in design and consisted of only short interviews with a small number of participants. Some cultural differences were observed between participants and it was not clear whether the results would generalise to a larger sample. Therefore, a large-scale quantitative study and a pilot were designed to explore the themes that arose in the interviews in a larger sample. These are reported in the next chapter.

References

Adamson, S., & Holloway, M. (2012). A sound track of your life: Music in contemporary UK funerals. *OMEGA, 65*(1), 33–54.

Band At Funeral: Music Lover's Request. (1924, 8 August 1924). *The News*.

Braun, V., & Clarke, V. (2006). Using thematic analysis in psychology. *Qualitative Research in Psychology, 3*, 77–101.

Britten, N. (1995). Qualitative Research: Qualitative interviews in medical research. *British Medical Journal, 311*, 251–253.

Caswell, G. (2011–2012). Beyond words: Some uses of music in the funeral setting. *OMEGA: Journal of Death and Dying, 64*(4), 319–334.

Cook, G., & Walter, T. (2005). Rewritten rites: language and social relations in traditional and contemporary funerals. *Discourse and Society, 16*(3), 365–391.

Co-operative Funeralcare (2013). Funeral Music. Retrieved from http://www.co-operative.coop/funeralcare/arranging-a-funeral/your-guide-to-arranging-a-funeral/Funeral-Music/

Creswell, J. W., Plano Clark, V. L., Gutmann, M. L., & Hanson, W. E. (2003). Advanced mixed methods research designs. In A. Tashakkori & C. Teddlie (Eds.), *Handbook of Mixed Methods in Social & Behavioral Research* (pp. 209–240): Los Angeles: SAGE.

Floyd, A. E. (1936). Commemorative music: Funeral marches, *The Australasian* (2 May).

Gammon, V. (1988). Singing and popular funeral practices in the eighteenth and nineteenth centuries. *Folk Music Journal, 5*(4), 412–447.

Indian Hawker's Will. (1933). *The Courier Mail*. Retrieved from http://nla.gov.au/nla.news-article96088248

Indian Hawker's Will: Suitable Music for Funeral. *Recorder*. (1933). (8 November).

Johnson, R. B., Onwuegbuzie, A. J., & Turner, L. A. (2007). Toward a definition of mixed methods research. *Journal of Mixed Methods Research, 1*, 112–133.

Jupp, J. (2002). *The Australian People: An Encyclopedia of the Nation, Its People and Their Origins*. Cambridge: Cambridge University Press.

Kelton, S., & Steward, F. (2008). Queen, Led Zeppelin and AC/DC now Popular Funeral Songs. *The Daily Telegraph, July 02*. Retrieved from http://www.dailytelegraph.com.au/news/weird/queen-led-zeppelin-and-acdc-now-popular-funeral-songs/story-e6frev20-1111116793918

Late Bramwell Booth. (1929). *Singleton Argus* (21 June).

Leaver, R. A. (2002). Brahms's Opus 45 and German Protestant funeral music. *The Journal of Musicology, 19*(4), 616–640.

Meyers, K., Golden, R. N., & Peterson, F. (2009). *The Truth about Death and Dying*: Infobase Publishing.

Miles, M. B., & Huberman, A. M. (1994). *Qualitative Data Analysis: an Expanded Sourcebook* (2nd ed.). Thousand Oaks, CA.: Sage.

Parsons, B. (2012). Identifying key changes: The progress of cremation and its influence on music at funerals in England, 1874–2010. *Mortality, 17*(2), 130–144.

TGR. (1910). MUSIC, *The Queenslander,* p. 20. Retrieved from http://nla.gov.au/nla.news-article21881817

Whitwell, D. (n.d.). Funeral music in the ancient world. *Essays on the Origins of Western Music, 59*. Retrieved from http://www.whitwellessays.com/index.asp

3 The Modern Funeral and Music for Celebration

Part II

Sandra Garrido and Jane W. Davidson

Introduction

The music that people choose to play at funerals provides an interesting reflection of attitudes towards death and grief in society at large. The previous chapter (Part I) briefly outlined funeral music choices in European (primarily British) history, demonstrating that religious music and classical music were the most predominant choices. Music at funerals was also overwhelmingly mournful in character. However, in the first half of the twentieth century we see rituals of mourning in Western countries taking on new shapes. While choices were still necessarily limited by what was musically available, personal choice and the idea of celebrating the life of the deceased rather than focusing on loss began to have an influence on what music was played.

We argued at the close of the previous chapter that three main motivations for funeral music choices had emerged: following tradition, personal expression and mood creation. However, individual differences were clearly discernible even in the small sample used in the study in Part I. Therefore, these three themes were used as the basis for creating a survey questionnaire to further investigate these motivations in a larger sample. With the studies reported in this chapter we wanted to further explore the tension between 'appropriateness' and the need for personal expression in funerals as illustrated by music choices. We also wanted to test the extent to which the desire to create a certain mood would motivate funeral music choices and to find out whether participants feel that a mournful atmosphere should be created.

The large-scale survey reported in this chapter relates to data collected from a website[1] called *My Life As A Playlist*, a project running in collaboration between the Australian Research Council Centre of Excellence for the History of Emotions and the Australian Broadcasting Corporation (ABC). The content of the website includes quizzes and detailed surveys procuring information on how and why people regulate mood using music in their lives – especially around ceremonies such as falling in love, special birthday celebrations, marriage and funerals.

---

1 www.abc.net.au/playlist

Pilot Study

In preparation for the large-scale questionnaire that formed part of the ABC website, we piloted a survey about funeral music choices with 227 undergraduate students from a university in Australia, many of whom were music students. The participants were mostly in the 18–25 age group and included 85 males and 140 females (gender information was missing for 2 participants). Participants were questioned about general music listening preferences and habits as well as musical experience, and then were asked to nominate a piece of music (and its composer or performer) that they would choose to be played at their funeral. They were then asked to select the reason they selected this music from a list of eight options, the final one of which was labelled 'other' and allowed the participant to give additional reasons if they were not covered in the previous options. These items were designed to explore the three main motivations derived from the previous study: following tradition, creating a certain mood or emotion, and expressing something personal. Some of the options included in the list were 'It is traditionally played at funerals in my culture', 'This music represents how I would like people to remember me', and 'For humour or irony'.

Since we also wanted to find out whether the desire to create a certain mood or emotional state in funeral attenders was a motivating factor, it was necessary not only to question participants as to the reasons for their choices, but to find out whether they viewed the music they were choosing as sad or happy. For example, some traditional songs such as 'Amazing Grace' or 'Danny Boy' can be performed various ways so as to convey differing emotions. The final question allowed participants to rate the music they had chosen using a sliding bar to indicate the valence[2] of the music (1 = a negative emotion like sadness or anger, 5 = a positive emotion like happiness or peacefulness).

The music nominated by participants that they would play at their funeral was categorised into genres. In order to do this we collected 'tags' from the online music service Last.fm. Tags are 'free-form labels or key-words collaboratively applied to documents by users in online services' (Saari & Eerola, 2013, p. 1). The resulting meta-data has been found to be useful in various kinds of analyses, including studies looking at lyric content and mood (Saari & Eerola, 2013) as well as genre classification (Chen, Wright & Nejdl, 2009). It has been found to be a useful alternative to audio analysis or manual categorisation by experts as a method of genre classification (Chen, Wright & Nejdl, 2009). However, one limitation of this method for genre classification is that users sometimes assign multiple tags to a song, so implying different

---

2 Valence is one of two dimensions (arousal being the other) by which emotion theorists in psychology categorise emotions. It refers to the intrinsic aversiveness or attractiveness (pleasantness or unpleasantness) of the emotion. For example, emotions with a negative valence include 'unpleasant' emotions such as anger and fear which tend to stimulate avoidance behaviours, while emotions of a positive valence include 'pleasant' emotions such as joy or peace which tend to stimulate approach behaviours.

20 *Sandra Garrido and Jane W. Davidson*

genres. In order to overcome the problem, we decided to classify the songs in genre clusters rather than in individual genres. Our clusters were based upon the visualisation produced by Saari and Eerola (2013). Those authors focused on Rock, Pop, Electronic, Metal, Jazz and Folk and clustered various sub-genres derived from social tags under those labels. Since our sample included more than just popular music genres we added a 'Classical' cluster that broadly included classical music, other instrumental music and soundtracks. We also wanted to separately look at other non-classical funeral music choices, so we added the categories 'Traditional/Sacred', and 'Humorous', resulting in a total of nine genre clusters.

Results

The most popular choice of genre for the participants in this study was pop music (39.6%) with classical music being the second most popular choice (27.4%). Traditional choices including hymns like 'Amazing Grace' (1779), religious music from non-Christian faiths, contemporary Christian songs or other commonly used songs such as 'Danny Boy' (1913) were less common (14.1%). These results are not surprising given the relatively young age of our participants, and suggest that traditional choices are of lesser importance and meaning to young people than popular music. Nevertheless, traditional choices were still nominated by a number of participants. The fact that classical music also received a relatively high nomination rate was likely due to the fact that many of the participants were undergraduate music students. In fact, statistical analysis revealed that musical experience was a significant predictor of the genre of music chosen, with people who described themselves as 'consumers' only of music (as opposed to people who played an instrument or sang), more likely to choose popular music, while people who described themselves as professional musicians or music students were most likely to choose classical music.

The majority of participants selected music that they rated as having a positive valence (67.8%). Approximately one fifth chose music of a negative valence and the rest rated their choice as being of neutral valence. Thus, it is evident that most people did not nominate 'mournful' music for their own funeral, but preferred music expressing positive emotions.

The most frequently reported motivation for selecting the nominated music for their funeral was that the music expressed the participant's ideals about life and death (see Table 3.1 in the Appendix). Other popular reasons were that the participant liked features of the music itself or that it reminded them of special times in their lives. Choice of music because it was mournful and therefore appropriate to a funeral setting accounted for only 9.9% of participants. Similarly, choice of music because it was traditional represented only 4.2% of participants. Some of the reasons given by participants who selected the 'other' option were that the song was a 'favourite', that the participant liked the lyrics, to 'inspire others to find God', so that family and friends would be relaxed and would not cry, or because the music was important for family reasons. These findings were in

The Modern Funeral and Music for Celebration: Part II   21

support of our hypothesis that for the majority of participants the expression of something personal would be a greater motivation than following tradition.

We then conducted statistical analyses to see whether there was any relationship between the chosen genre and the motivation given for the choice. As would be expected, people for whom tradition was important were more likely to choose music from the Traditional/Sacred classification than others. Conversely, people who chose music because it represented how they wanted to be remembered were less likely to choose Traditional/Sacred music than other groups and generally chose music of a more positive valence than others. Classical music was the most prevalent choice for people who felt mournful music was the most appropriate, while people who wanted to express humour or irony in their choice most frequently nominated popular music.

These results suggest that for the relatively young sample in this study, the following of tradition was of less importance than personal meaning and expression, and that traditional and sacred songs held minimal personal meaning for the majority. The young people in this group preferred to express positive emotions than mournful ones in their music selections, and were concerned about leaving positive memories behind them. However, the results also revealed that for some young people traditional choices and classical music were still important. The larger scale website created in collaboration with the ABC would recruit participants from more varied age groups and ranges of musical experience to test the applicability of these findings to the general population.

The Large-Scale Study

In this next phase of our research we also wanted to explore whether any particular personality factors were associated with the importance an individual gave to following tradition. We hypothesised that a nostalgic longing for the past might cause an individual to value music of the past more than people who tend to be future-oriented. *The New Oxford Dictionary of English* ('Nostalgia', 1998) defines nostalgia as 'a sentimental longing or wistful affection for the past'. One of the psychological functions which nostalgia is believed to fulfil is the need to interpret and recover the past (Cassia, 2000). This yearning for the ideal of the past can be both a yearning for past stages of one's own life (personal nostalgia), or for past historical periods through which one has not necessarily lived (historical nostalgia) (Holbrook, 1993; Marchegiani & Phau, 2011). It can be an effective way to cope with discontinuity or existential threat such as that caused by migration or family break-up (Sedikides *et al.*, 2010). We therefore decided to investigate whether or not a proneness to personal or historical nostalgia could be related to a tendency to make traditional choices when it comes to funeral music.

Coping style is also closely related to how people deal with issues like grief and death in their own lives. Research on coping styles indicates that how a person habitually responds to stressful events can influence their use of music in those circumstances. Garrido and Schubert (2011, 2013a), for example, found that people with ruminative or reflective coping styles tend to be attracted to sad music

22   *Sandra Garrido and Jane W. Davidson*

when experiencing negative emotions. Miranda and Claes (2009) report finding three styles of coping that directly involved music: emotion-oriented, problem-oriented and avoidance/disengagement. Therefore, we hoped that the inclusion of some measure of coping styles in the current study might further illuminate the way personality could influence music choices for funerals.

We were able to recruit 433 participants through the *My Life As A Playlist* website, including 297 females, 131 males and 2 'others' (3 people did answer the question) with a mean age of 35.6 years (range 15–83). We used a refined version of the survey used in the pilot, with the added inclusion of the Rumination Reflection Questionnaire RRQ; Trapnell & Campbell, 1999), the Coping Orientations to Problems Experienced scale (COPE; Carver, Scheier & Weintraub, 1989), a measure of personal nostalgia Batcho's Nostalgia Inventory (Batcho's Nostalgia Inventory; Batcho, 1995) and one of historical nostalgia (Holbrook, 1993), as well as the Big Five Inventory (BFI; John & Srivastava, 1999).

Participants were asked to name a piece of music that they would play at their own funeral and to choose the most applicable option from a list of 12 motivations which were a modification and expansion of the similar items in the pilot study (see Table 3.2 in the Appendix). Similarly to the pilot study, ratings of the selected music were given on dimensions of valence and arousal.[3] Since we particularly wanted to gauge participants' response to and liking for a 'traditional' choice of music for a funeral, participants listened to the first movement of Mozart's Requiem ('Introitus') and were told that this was played at the funeral of Napoleon Bonaparte. They were then asked whether or not they would play this music at their funeral and were able to choose the most applicable item from a number of options to explain why or why not. Participants answered a similar series of questions about music they would choose for the funeral of another person as well as to indicate whether the funeral they were imagining was that of a spouse, parent, sibling, friend or other family member.

The music nominated by participants was classified in genre clusters as in the pilot study using four meta-clusters: Traditional/Sacred, Popular (including pop, rock, electronic etc.), Instrumental/Classical (which also included jazz) and Humorous. Based on findings in our previous study, we also allocated items relating to the motivation for choices into clusters which included: Following Tradition, Personal Expression, Aesthetic Reasons and Mood Creation.

Results

Popular music was the most frequently chosen genre for both one's own funeral and for the funeral of another, with Instrumental/Classical rating second highest.

---

3   Arousal is the other dimension commonly used in emotion categorisation in addition to valence, and refers to the energy level of the music. For example, low arousal emotions tend to be low energy emotions such as sadness and peacefulness, while high arousal emotions can include emotions such as anger and happiness.

The Modern Funeral and Music for Celebration: Part II   23

Traditional/Sacred choices and Humorous had the lowest ratings. This replicated the results of the pilot study despite the differing demographics of the samples. However, statistical analysis revealed that genre choice was related to age, with the mean age of people who chose popular music (33.9 years) being significantly lower than those who chose Instrumental/Classical (42.2 years). However, age was not significantly different for people who chose Traditional/Sacred music, suggesting that it is of equal importance for all age groups. The music selected was again of predominantly positive valence and relatively high arousal, indicating that the music selected expressed mostly positive emotions of high energy such as joy or elation. The selection of music of negative valence was associated with the Big Five personality item of Neuroticism, while selecting music of a positive valence was related to the trait of Conscientiousness.

Personal Expression was again the paramount reason given for the music selections for both one's own funeral and for the funeral of another. The most frequently selected motivation for the music nominated for one's own funeral was 'The music expresses what I want to say'. Similarly, in relation to the music chosen for the funeral of another, the importance the music had to the individual for whose funeral it would be used was the most highly rated item. Participant responses to the excerpt played from Mozart's Requiem reflected similar thinking. The majority said they would not use music from the Requiem for their own funeral (88.7%), with the primary reason given being that they would prefer to use music that meant something to them personally and that Mozart held little meaning for them personally and did not reflect their own personality or beliefs. Of those who said they would use it for their own funeral, the most frequently selected reason was that it was appropriately mournful.

When we analysed scores on the personality scales we found that people who chose Traditional/Sacred music had significantly higher scores on the Religious Coping subscale than people who chose popular music. On the other hand, people who chose Popular music had significantly higher scores on the Coping by Humour subscale than those who chose Traditional/Sacred music. Personal nostalgia levels were higher for people who selected music for specific Mood Creation reasons than for people whose motivation was Personal Expression. These results suggest that music choices offer an interesting reflection of coping styles.

Discussion

In the series of studies conducted in both Part I and Part II we were interested in finding out what kind of music people would choose to play at funerals in modern times, given the increasingly personalised options that are available to them. We also wanted to find out what might motivate such choices, and in particular, the extent to which tradition would be an influence. Of further interest was how personality and coping style might also be related to the choices people would make about music use at funerals. The initial qualitative phase (reported in Part I) found that both personal expression and tradition were of importance to participants as was the desire to celebrate life. We followed this up with two quantitative studies

24   Sandra Garrido and Jane W. Davidson

(Part II) designed to further investigate these motivations in relation to both one's own funeral and that of a loved one.

The pilot study involving a student sample revealed that popular music was the genre of choice for most young people in the study. However, Traditional/ Sacred and Instrumental/Classical were surprisingly highly rated given the youthfulness of the sample. The connection between age and genre was further explored in the large-scale study, where we found that Popular music was most often chosen by younger participants while older participants were more likely to choose instrumental or classical music. However, Traditional/Sacred choices were more evenly spread across the age groups. This tends to confirm what seems intuitive: that is, that genre choices relate to age. However, it seems that traditional and sacred music are still of importance to many people whatever their age may be.

In the qualitative study reported in the previous chapter (Part I) nearly all participants mentioned the concept of joy and celebration or the desire to 'leave them laughing' and not 'grieving too much'. The fact that many people do not want to use music that is overly sad was further confirmed in both the pilot and the large-scale study reported in this chapter, with the choice of music of a pre-dominantly positive valence. Interestingly, however, this appears to be related to personality. The Big Five trait of Conscientiousness was predictive of choosing music of a positive valence for one's own funeral. Conscientious people are highly thoughtful of other people and are characterised by a strong motivation to act dutifully (Goldberg, 1990; Gosling, Rentfrow & Swann, 2003). It may be that it is such thoughtfulness that might motivate an individual to choose music that would not cause the mourners to be too emotionally weighed down. On the other hand, highly neurotic people were more likely to choose negatively valenced music, a finding that tends to support the idea that sad music is often utilised as part of maladaptive strategies for coping with stresses such as grief (Garrido, 2009; Garrido & Schubert, 2013b).

To the three primary motivations for music choices for one's own funeral identified in our previous research – the desire to follow tradition, to create a specific mood or atmosphere and to express something personal – we were able to add a fourth motivation: aesthetics. The most frequent motivation for the music chosen was to express something personal, whether that is one's own personality, beliefs and values, memories, or life experiences, or the personality and experiences of another person whose funeral was being considered. Following tradition was a much less significant motivation to most people. When personal expression was the primary motivation, Traditional/Sacred music was much less likely to be the chosen music. The overall rejection of the historical excerpt from Mozart's Requiem which was played to participants and the primary moti-vation given for rejecting it (that it is not personally relevant) tend to confirm these findings.

Again the motivations for choices appear to be related to personality and coping style. People with a religious coping style were more likely to choose

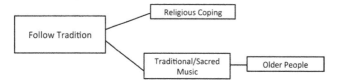

Figure 3.1 Personal variables and music choices for following tradition motivation

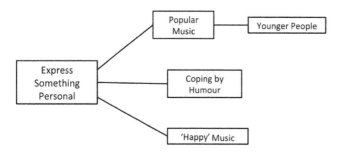

Figure 3.2 Personal variables and music choices for personal expression motivation

traditional music and not popular (see Figure 3.1). Conversely, people with strong scores in coping with humour were more likely to choose popular music than traditional (see Figure 3.2). People whose motivation was primarily aesthetic tended to prefer sad music (see Figure 3.3), while people with high scores in nostalgia-proneness often made music choices based on the desire to create a certain mood whether happy or sad (Figure 3.4). Nostalgia is typically described as 'bittersweet' since it can involve both the pleasant remembrance of times past along with the painful realisation that the past is gone forever (Davidson & Garrido, 2014). The findings in this study that the choice of sad music is predominantly associated with neuroticism while choosing happy music is related to the psychologically healthier trait of conscientiousness, tends to reflect the mixed emotions associated with nostalgia and perhaps further suggest that music can have mixed psychological outcomes on people who choose it for its nostalgic value.

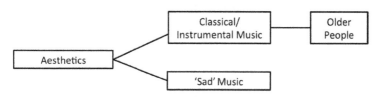

Figure 3.3 Personal variables and music choices for aesthetic motivation

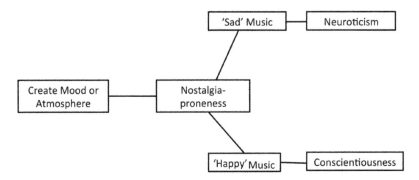

Figure 3.4 Personal variables and music choices for mood creation motivation

Although tradition was still important to some participants, for the majority, traditional choices did not coincide with their desire to portray their own values and ideals in a funeral setting. Wouters (2002) describes mourning in many countries as being 'poised between a highly institutionalized social obligation and a highly individual and personal feeling, respectively a public and a private process' (p. 1). Adamson and Holloway (2012) similarly report the important role that music played in the funerals they studied in creating both a sense of public ceremony as well as a 'personal existential quest' (p. 33). This tension between tradition and appropriateness, and personal expression was also reflected in the results of our study.

Thus, although one participant in the study reported in Part I expressed the concern that her personal choices might not be 'allowed' in a church, many people appear to be finding a way to create personalised expressions through music, even in traditional settings (Cook & Walter, 2005; Garces-Foley & Holcomb, 2005). This embodies an attempt to combine old and new ideals and to create ways of mourning that are a compromise between tradition and modern ideals of self-expression (Kotthoff, 2006).

Of course, for a number of people for whom personal expression is the primary motivation, traditional/sacred music may still hold personal meaning. In such cases, the choices of traditional music in modern times are most likely freely made to express religious beliefs or other values, rather than being dictated by custom or procedure. The results also indicate that, despite Australia being a largely secular culture (Jalland, 2006), religious faiths are still a consolation to some in the face of death. In addition to those who nominated traditional songs as their choice (including religious music of both Christian and non-Christian faiths), a number of participants in Part II selected Christian pop music or other contemporary Christian songs, reflecting the revival of evangelical Protestant churches such as 'Hillsong' in this country (Connell, 2005; Jennings, 2008). These songs often tend to be positive in valence or even celebratory, in light of the hope that they express of an afterlife. The predominantly positive music chosen by participants suggests that for the majority, celebration is preferred to focusing on loss. However, people with tendencies to neuroticism, which is linked to depression and maladaptive coping strategies (Thompson, 2008), were more likely to choose 'sad' music, suggesting a link between music choices and coping styles.

Although this study was limited by the fact that it focused on the contemplation of hypothetical situations, the connections found between music choices and coping styles implies that the choosing of music for the funeral of a loved one or for one's own funeral may form a useful part of the process of adjustment in situations of grief. For the participants in our studies people with a Religious or Humorous coping style – both considered healthy ways of dealing with adversity – music was able to provide an expression of this way of coping. However, the implications of this study also suggest that music can be an expression of unhealthy ways of coping. These findings are highly relevant for the many people such as chaplains, funeral directors or counsellors seeking to help those grieving to find appropriate ways of coping with their loss. For people who are facing death, such as those in palliative care or the very elderly, the contemplation of their funeral music choices could also be a useful tool for dealing with anticipatory grief that has not always been available in previous time periods when music choices were less flexible. The selection of music can provide an opportunity for people to reflect on their lives (Aldridge, 1999; Magee & Davidson, 2004), to celebrate it and to be remembered in the way that they personally choose. It also offers an opportunity for them to demonstrate their concern for how those left behind will cope. Some appear to prefer to use this chance to give the gift of joy and laughter one last time.

Further research on this topic would benefit from considering how older populations or those with terminal illnesses make decisions about the music they would like at their funeral. It would also be useful to investigate further whether such populations derive any comfort from the process of contemplation and selection. Nevertheless, what is clear from this study is that music choices serve as a fascinating reflection of attitudes to life and death in society and how we deal with grief and loss. Music is therefore an important aspect of funeral practices in coming to an understanding of death and mourning in contemporary Western culture.

Appendix

Table 3.1 Survey options for reason for funeral music choice and percentage of participants who selected them in the pilot study

Item Number		Percentage of Participants
FM1	It is traditionally played at funerals in my culture	4.2
FM2	It expresses my personal ideals about life and death	21.6
FM3	This music represents how I would like people to remember me	12.2
FM4	It brings back memories of some special times in my life	13.6
FM5	The music is mournful and seems suited to a funeral	9.9
FM6	I am attracted to some of the features of the music (e.g. the singer, the rhythm, the instruments)	16.4
FM7	For humour or irony	8.0
FM8	Other. Please give details	14.1

Table 3.2 Survey options for reason for funeral music choice and Reason Cluster in the large-scale study

Item Number		Reason Cluster
FMR1	It's traditional to play this music at funerals. It feels right.	Traditional
FMR2	This music expresses what I want to say.	Personal
FMR3	It's so me – just how I'd like to be remembered.	Personal
FMR4	Some of my favourite memories flood back when I hear this.	Personal
FMR5	It's sad – I can imagine it being played at a funeral.	Mood
FMR6	Elements of the music resonate with me (e.g. the rhythm, the instruments, the voice).	Aesthetic
FMR7	It reflects my sense of humour. I want people to remember me with laughter and love!	Mood
FMR8	I used to perform this piece of music.	Personal
FMR9	My funeral wouldn't be complete without music from this artist – love them.	Aesthetic
FMR10	This piece has political or social message that is important to me.	Personal
FMR11	I love this era – this music makes me feel like I've travelled back in time.	Traditional
FMR12	It's part of my culture, and heritage is important to me.	Traditional

References

Adamson, S., & Holloway, M. (2012). A sound track of your life: Music in contemporary UK funerals. *OMEGA, 65*(1), 33–54.

Aldridge, D. (1999). *Music Therapy in Palliative Care: New Voices*. London: Jessica Kingsley Publishers.

Batcho, K. I. (1995). Nostalgia: A psychological perspective. *Perceptual and Motor Skills, 80*, 131–143.

Carver, C. S., Scheier, M. F., & Weintraub, J. K. (1989). Assessing coping strategies: A theoretically based approach. *Journal of Personality and Social Psychology, 56*, 267–283.

Cassia, P. S. (2000). Exoticizing discoveries and extraordinary experiences: 'Traditional' music, modernity, and nostalgia in Malta and other Mediterranean societies. *Ethnomusicology, 44*(2), 281–301.

Chen, L., Wright, P., & Nejdl, W. (2009). *Improving music genre classification using collaborative tagging data.* Paper presented at the Second ACM Interational Conference on Web Search and Data Mining, Barcelona, Spain.

Connell, J. (2005). Hillsong: A megachurch in the Sydney suburbs. *Australian Geographer, 36*(3), 315–332.

Davidson, J., & Garrido, S. (2014). *My Life As A Playlist*. Perth: University of Western Australia Publishing.

Garces-Foley, K., & Holcomb, J. S. (2005). Personalizing Tradition. In K. Garces-Foley (Ed.), *Death and Religion in a Changing World*. Armonk, NY: M. E. Sharpe.

Garrido, S. (2009). Rumination and sad music: A review of the literature and a future direction. In Catherine Stevens, E. Schubert, B. Kruithof, K. Buckley & S. Fazio (Eds.), *Proceedings of the 2nd International Conference on Music Communication Science (ICoMCS2)* (pp. 20–23). Sydney: HCSNet, University of Western Sydney.

Garrido, S., & Schubert, E. (2011). Individual differences in the enjoyment of negative emotion in music: A literature review and experiment. *Music Perception, 28*(3), 279–295.

Garrido, S., & Schubert, E. (2013a). Adaptive and maladaptive attraction to negative emotion in music. *Musicae Scientiae, 17*(2), 145–164.

Garrido, S., & Schubert, E. (2013b). Moody melodies: Do they cheer us up? A study of the effect of sad music on mood. *Psychology of Music, 43*(2), 244–261.

Goldberg, L. R. (1990). An alternative 'description of personality': The Big-Five factor structure. *Journal of Personality and Social Psychology, 59*(6), 1,216–1,229.

Gosling, S. D., Rentfrow, P. J., & Swann, W. B. (2003). A very brief measure of the Big-Five personality domains. *Journal of Research in Personality, 37*, 504–528.

Holbrook, M. B. (1993). Nostalgia and consumption preferences: Some emerging patterns of consumer tastes. *Journal of Consumer Research, 20*, 245–256.

Jalland, P. (2006). *Changing ways of death in twentieth-century Australia: war, medicine and the funeral business*. Sydney: UNSW Press.

Jennings, M. (2008). 'Won't you break free?' An ethnography of music and the divine-human encounter at an Australian Pentecostal church. *Culture and Religion: An Interdisciplinary Journal, 9*(2), 161–174.

John, O. P., & Srivastava, S. (1999). The Big Five trait taxonomy: History, measurement and theoretical perspective. In L. A. Pervin & O. P. John (Eds.), *Handbook of personality: Theory and research* (2nd ed., pp. 102–138). New York: Guildford Press.

Kotthoff, H. (2006). Communicating affect in intercultural lamentations in Caucasian Georgia. In K. Buhrig & J. D. T. Thije (Eds.), *Beyond Misunderstanding: Linguistic Analyses of Intercultural Communication*. Amsterdam: John Benjamins Publishing.

30 *Sandra Garrido and Jane W. Davidson*

Magee, W. L., & Davidson, J. W. (2004). Music therapy in Multiple Sclerosis: Results of a systematic qualitative analysis. *Music Therapy Perspectives, 22*(1), 39–51.

Marchegiani, C., & Phau, I. (2011). The value of historical nostalgia for marketing management. *Marketing Intelligence and Planning, 29*(2), 108–122.

Miranda, D., & Claes, M. (2009). Music listening, coping, peer affiliation and depression in adolescence. *Psychology of Music, 37*(2), 215–233.

'Nostalgia'. (1998) *The New Oxford Dictionary of English.* Oxford: Oxford University Press.

Saari, P., & Eerola, T. (2013). Semantic computing of moods based on tags in social media of music. *IEEE Transactions on Knowledge and Data Engineering, 01 Aug.*

Sedikides, C., Wildschut, T., Gaertner, L., Routledge, C., & Arndt, J. (2010). Nostalgia as enabler of self-continuity. In F. Sani (Ed.), *Self Continuity: Individual and Collective Perspectives.* New York: Psychology Press.

Thompson, E. R. (2008). Development and validation of an International English Big Five Mini-Markers. *Personality and Individual Differences, 45*(6), 542–548.

Wouters, C. (2002). The quest for new rituals in dying and mourning: Changes in the we-I balance. *Body and Society, 8*(1), 1–27.

4 'The Ceremony of Tolling the Bell at the Time of Death'

Bell-ringing and Mourning in England c.1500–c.1700

Dolly MacKinnon

Introduction

In early modern England bells announced the cycles of life and death. Bells regulated the seasons, and also through their sounds or silences articulated the religious and political adherences of individual parish communities across the city, towns and countryside. In rural and urban settings all those who lived within earshot of church towers knew the particular sounds of their parish bells or bell. The tolling of bells for the dead was especially poignant, and specific bells were reserved for this function. 'The Ceremony of Tolling the Bell at the Time of Death, seems to be as ancient as the having of Bells themselves', wrote Henry Bourne in 1725 (p. 2). His publication had set out the *Antiquities Vulgares; or, the Antiquities of the Common People. Giving account of Several of their opinions and ceremonies with Proper reflections upon each of them; shewing which may be retain'd and which ought to be laid aside.* The 'Reason why this Custom was instituted', Bourne added, 'was not as some seem to imagine, for no other End than to acquaint the Neighbourhood, that such a Person was dead; but chiefly, that whoever heard the Noise of the Bell should put up their Prayers for the Soul' (1725, p.2). The sound of a bell tolling was therefore understood to be connected with the spiritual and emotional world of the parish whether or not the individual listener agreed with the practice. For early modern England (c.1500–c.1700), as David Cressy (1999, p. 421) has concluded, 'parish bells tolled when a person was dying, then signaled that someone was dead, and often rang again at the time of their burial'. And what is more, 'sometimes the bells sounded for hours on end, ringing both day and night' (1999, p. 421).

The bell tolling then forms part of the particular norms of emotional expression that each 'emotional community' (Rosenwein, 2006) performed through their specific use of the death knell. This definition derives from Barbara Rosenwein's conception of *Emotional Communities* (2006) that use a common emotional language and syntax. Here I have extended this to include a musical language represented by forms of bell tolling for the dead by adapting Jacques Attali's *Noise: The Political Economy of Music* (1985), which theorizes that communities purposefully identified the boundaries of their musical worlds by isolating, categorizing, and classifying sounds while rejecting noises. By applying

32   Dolly MacKinnon

this conceptualization it is possible to demonstrate the early modern norms of emotional communities' expressions of the death knell in the two case-study examples I discuss.

The intentional use of bell sounds and the reaction to them in the context of death rituals fits this model very well. The soundscape of mourning in seventeenth-century England was awash with the emotional connections and exclusions that bell soundwaves both generated and breached. By recasting and incorporating Attali's concept of noise, combined with Rosenwein's emotional communities, into an early modern soundscape of seventeenth-century England, we can identify the collision points of the sonic boundaries of acceptability and deviation recorded in the tangible archival traces of accounts regarding the ringing for the dead. 'Emotional communities' were made up of like-minded individuals who collectively identified sounds while rejecting noises.

These collision points occur where one community's death knell might be heard simultaneously by another emotional community as a jangling of bells; a noise that sat outside the boundaries of their perceptions of acceptable mourning. Here I will very briefly analyse the complex place of the emotional language of bell-ringing for the dead in England between c.1500 and c.1700, using two examples at the extremities of the early modern soundscape of tolling bells. Utilizing archival evidence that focuses on one auditory aspect of early modern England, these two case studies demonstrate the emotional power of bells either through their absence or purposeful ringing for the dead. Bell-ringing could simultaneously unite and divide parishes, as the performance of the ritual sounds of death, burial and mourning, were particular to each emotional community.

While much has been written about campanology, especially in the nineteenth century, bell-ringing in general in early modern England has been the focus of only a few important studies by David Cressy (1989, 1999), Christopher Marsh (2010), and David Postles (2006). My own work in the area of soundscape studies (MacKinnon, 2007, 2014), and the work of Bruce Smith (1999) for early modern London, and David Garrioch (2003) for cities in early modern Europe, situate their work within the long standing interdisciplinary historiographical tradition pioneered by Richard Murray Schafer (1977). None of these studies, however, has considered the emotional world of the sounds of bell ringing, and therefore for the purposes of this chapter I will turn my attention to the dimension of bells rung in mourning.

Seventeenth-century England was still in the grips of an ongoing Reformation surrounding the ritual practices of religion in urban and rural parishes across the country. The unifying and disparate ways in which different groups of parishioners might understand the spiritual significance of the sound of the bells they generated, heard or ignored, allows us to think of these groups not only in terms of musical communities, but also as emotional communities. These emotional communities experienced a physical emotional response to a tolling bell's sound wave. The reality of early modern parish communities was that they heard inclusions and exclusions, and this model offers us a substantial way forward in understanding these boundaries and breaches. A tolling bell could be both a unifying sound, as well as a fracture point in parish soundscapes. The presence or absence of a tolling bell at the time of death or burial evident in my two case studies from post-Reformation England demonstrates how certain members of communities either purposely reflected or rejected what communities considered an appropriate form of ringing for the dead in early seventeenth-century Protestant England.

Within certain English parishes, what was deemed appropriate by one group of parishioners may have proved highly contentious for a different parish group or groups. Within Protestantism, the use and function of bells engendered conflicting responses. While restrained use of bells could call the faithful to prayer, for others only the complete cessation of these sounds was acceptable. As one seventeenth-century English Protestant minister proclaimed, bells represented the corruption of an idolatrous and unreformed church, describing bell towers as 'these old Chyming chimneys of the drunken whore of *Babylon*' and indicative of 'The Peoples Idols-Temples-Steeples-Bells' and the noise of an unreformed soundscape (Chidley, 1656, pamphlet). Chidley's biblical reference to the whore of Babylon riding the seven-headed beast comes from Revelations, and was a common symbol used by Protestants from the Lutheran Reformation onwards to describe the Roman Catholic Church as the anti-Christ. As David Garrioch has observed for early modern cities in Europe, parish bells created 'local "sound-marks"' (Truax, 1984, p. 76; Garrioch, 2003, p. 14). Garrioch builds on the work of Barry Truax, who conceptualized societies as comprising 'acoustic communities' (Truax, 1984, pp. 76–77). Within cities then, there were 'overlapping acoustic communities' where 'those who belonged to a particular neighborhood recognized its sounds and responded in ways outsiders did not' (Garrioch, 2003, p. 14). Certain sounds and the responses they elicited in the listeners constructed 'different acoustic communities associated not only with particular areas but also with specific cultural, religious and ethnic groups' (Garrioch, 2003, pp. 15–16). And to extend this to its natural conclusion, those ritual sounds manifest themselves in the emotional connection forged between mourning and the specific pitches of certain bells used to herald this occurrence to the ears of the parish.

At the Reformation, Protestantism abolished purgatory, that state of suffering where souls lingered after death, and from which the sinner might have their journey to heaven, rather than to hell, secured by the purchase of indulgences, and prayers for the dead. Pre-Reformation tolling for the dying and dead purposefully called the listeners to pray for those souls in purgatory in order to assist their progress, towards heaven. After the abolition of purgatory, Protestants, instead of silencing the tolling bell now implored the listeners to reflect on the life and piety of the deceased, as well as reflect on the spirituality of their own lives. David Cressy (1999, p. 396) has observed 'one of the most profound effects of the protestant elimination of purgatory' at the time of the English Reformation in the sixteenth century, and its ongoing rippling effects into the seventeenth century, was its capacity 'to shrink the community of souls and to sever the relationship between the living and the dead'. No longer could the living assist the dead. While this curtailed bell-ringing for the dead it did not silence it. Central to this shift was the perceived change of the purpose and function of the death knell that was

34   *Dolly MacKinnon*

tolled as one passed out of life, and the funeral bell that tolled at the burial. In England the Reformation saw many of the sounds of death removed and the 'trentals, masses, dirges, and prayers of the dead were resolutely set aside', for 'the souls of departed protestants were now thought to be beyond the reach of intersessionary prayer' (Cressy, 1999, p. 396). These forms of ringing were officially, if not actually, silenced. For Protestants the Roman Catholic soundmarks of tolling bells assisting the soul on its journey no longer held any theological justification. Yet the uptake of these Protestant reforms was neither uniform nor consistent across more than 9,000 parishes in England. Adherents to the old religion and the associated bell-ringing practices persisted, and the previous practices surrounding the ceremony of tolling for the dead rang on in Protestant England during the seventeenth century.

While some extreme Protestants wished to silence the passing bell, others wished simply to remove the superstition they considered was associated with it. For Roman Catholics, the bell was one of the mechanisms, including prayers for the dead, that assisted the soul on its journey through purgatory. The collision of these simultaneous understandings of the purpose and function of the passing bell is reflected in the following example from Durham. In the rules for funerals published posthumously by James Pilkington, bishop of Durham (1561–1576) in 1585, Pilkington stipulated that 'papists infinitely offend' through their insistence on performing 'masses, dirges, trenals, singing, ringing' amongst other superstitions, and his successor Bishop Richard Barnes, forbad 'any superfluous' ringing (Scholefield, 1842, pp. 318 & 543 cited in Cressy, 1999, p. 399).

While proscriptions prevailed, practices remained variable, as sections of Northern England remained staunchly Catholic in this now officially Protestant country. For example, late sixteenth–century Lancashire was, as Cressy (1999, p. 400) has concluded, a 'local culture in the midst of an uncomfortable transition'. Here we can read the reaction of one emotional community's response to the appropriate soundscape of death of the other, including a pejorative description that defined as noise the sounds of the centuries-old ritual trappings of Catholic England. In Catholic Lancashire 'the bells all the while being rung many a solemn peal' and at the burial of the dead 'another sort of jangling the bells'. As Cressy (1999, p. 402) concludes, 'a picture emerges of a hybrid religious culture, in which reformed and unreformed elements intermingled while being pressured towards conformity'. Accompanying this hybrid religious culture were the soundscapes of continuity and change. Let us now turn to the mourning bell-ringing practice used at the death of the openly Roman Catholic, Henry Howard, Lord Privy Seal during the reign of James VI & I in Protestant London in 1614.

Henry Howard (died 1614)

Bells accompanied Henry Howard, Lord Privy Seal, both in life and in death. He had taken the Oath of Allegiance (1606) that allowed Roman Catholics a religious freedom under James VI & I (Woodward, 1997, p. 144). His rank and position entitled him to his place in the early modern soundscape. In life and especially

'*The Ceremony of Tolling the Bell at the Time of Death*' 35

in death Howard's Roman Catholicism was audible, and at his burial there was a clear flaunting of Protestant England's auditory landscape through his 'popish' funeral and bell-ringing practices. The use of bells to announce the cycle of his life and death reflects the broader practice of bell sounds or silences articulating the religious and political adherences of individuals, as well as parish communities across the English landscapes. For example, at the death of either a Catholic or Protestant monarch bells would ring out across the parishes of England to herald national mourning in the sixteenth and seventeenth centuries. In rural and urban settings alike, all those who lived within earshot of church bell towers, and were familiar with the nuances of the bell sounds, knew the particular sound of their parish's death knell. For a monarch the bells would toll for free, but for everyone else these sounds of death and mourning were tolled for a fee, and were highly regulated. For example, at the death of Elizabeth I, when the bell tolled it resonated the status and funeral rituals befitting a monarch. The meaning of those specific sounds rung from one church and picked up and passed to the next was accompanied by the news these tolling bells heralded. Over the course of a number of hours, the death of Elizabeth I would have been communicated across the urban and rural landscape of England.

The death knell for the remainder of the population from aristocrats to artisans would have to be purchased in order for their own relative status to be publicly proclaimed from their parish bell tower across the village, town or cityscape. Only for the very wealthy or the very virtuous poor did a bell toll for free. In 1614, when Henry Howard, Lord Privy Seal and first Earl of Northampton, a Roman Catholic, lay mortally ill, he made arrangements for his Roman Catholic death and burial. He paid for his executors to ensure that 'a bell be tolled for one or two days prior to the funeral in loud contravention of the early Elizabethan [Protestant] pronouncements' which limited all but monarchy to a half-hour peel (Woodward, 1997, p. 144). Although Elizabeth was dead by 1614, the Protestant bell-ringing practice that she had instated and endorsed continued to gather momentum. The Gun Powder Plot of 1605, a Roman Catholic conspiracy to blow up the Houses of Parliament, hardened the resolve of the hotter sorts of Protestants with the public execution of the conspirators. Yet in 1611 James I & VI still complained 'about the number of people attending mass in the chapels of Catholic ambassadors' (1997, p. 144). As Woodward notes 'that the funeral [of Howard] was allowed to take place [in 1614] demonstrates that James . . . was careless about controlling the funeral rites of his subjects' (p. 144), In this case too, Howard's status as Lord Privy Seal and first Earl of Northampton placed him in the top echelon of Jacobean society.

The circumstances surrounding the events of Howard's death are recorded in a letter to Sir Dudley Carleton, penned by John Chamberlain in London, dated 30 June 1614. This letter archives the auditory realm of the early modern world in hints and snatches. In passing, Chamberlain noted that 'On Wensday in Whitson weeke the Lord Privie Seale, Henry Howard, first Earl of Northampton, departed this life, the same sevenight that he came through London as yt were in triumphe with only Sir Charles Cronwallis in his coach' (McClure, 1939, vol.1, pp. 540–544). That

36   *Dolly MacKinnon*

Howard 'came thorough London as yt were in triumphe' hints that he may also have been accompanied by the pealing of bells to accompany his progress through the city. This was a practice that was common and accompanied royalty and leading figures of aristocracy from the fifteenth century onwards in England for free, while for others wealthy enough they might purchase this soundmark for a fee. This brief account encompasses two occasions when the bells of London would have tolled for Henry Howard: bells pealed in his welcome to the parish, and bells tolled as part of the ritual of his dying, death and mourning in the early modern world. Here was a deeply held emotional response to death represented by the Roman Catholic practice of a tolling bell, a sound imbued with social, political and religious implications at odds with the Protestant understanding of a suitable soundscape for death and mourning.

The sequence of events surrounding Howard's illness and death enabled him to ensure his Roman Catholic provisions were in place. For as Chamberlain noted, 'he had a swelling in his thigh which increasing dayly, yt was thought goode after the applieng of mollifieng medicins to cut yt, whereupon yt grew so angrie that yt gangrened and made an end of him (McClure, 1939, vol. 1, pp. 540–544). That the infection in his leg claimed him rapidly is revealed by Chamberlain, who observed that 'Yt shold seeme the matter was very venomous when yt so poisoned Felton the surgeon that launct yt, that he hath ever since lien at deaths doore'. Howard, faced with impending death, may have heard Roman Catholic England through 'the bell hath tolled for him twise or thrise: and yt was very noiseome all the roome over a day or two before he died'. While an excess of bell tolling accompanied Henry Howard both out of life and to the grave in Protestant England, what of those for whom the bell rope stood still, and the bell remained silent? Let us now turn to the case of the death of the Dagenham Cobbler in Essex in 1606.

An Essex Cobbler (died 1606)

The absence and presence of bell sounds can be heard or not heard as an individual or collective religio-political 'soundmark' within and across emotional communities at particular points in time. In his magisterial study of *Birth, Marriage, and Death* (1999, p. 426) in Tudor and Stuart England, David Cressy briefly cited the case of a Cobbler from Dagenham, Essex. Discussed within the context of the ease with which early modern parish communities could dig a grave and accommodate another death even in 'waterlogged areas', Cressy cites this example from a partial nineteenth-century transcript of the early modern Archdeaconry accounts for Essex: 'One Christopher, a cobbler of Dagenham, Essex, was buried in 1606 within four hours of his dying. We know this because someone complained that he was buried in haste, "without any tolling of a bell, or any duty done by the minister".' Cressy offers no further analysis of this specific case, but observes that all burial and mourning practices were ranked against perceptions of 'human decency' and were a 'common concern' (Cressy, 1999, p. 426). The

'The Ceremony of Tolling the Bell at the Time of Death' 37

nineteenth-century transcription not discussed by Cressy must also attract a word of caution as well as word of explanation, for the partial transcription also hints at a darker sequence of events concerning the cobbler regarding the 'Burying without ceremony, and dividing the goods of the deceased', that are not born out by the early modern accounts. As such I shall be using a fuller transcription of the Archdeaconery Act Book Accounts for London held in the Essex Record Office (ERO D/AEA. 24).[1] If we take this example and continue the analysis beyond its brief use by Cressy, what might this case demonstrate about the emotional communities that were interlinked with the sounds and practices of mourning? What might it tell us about the events and circumstances that might mitigate or obfuscate the usual practices of religious emotional communities that tolled for their dead?

Let us turn to the version of events recounted in the Essex Record Office Transcription (ERO D/AEA. 24, p. 125 verso, Vol. IV folio 3) that sets out the sequence of events surrounding the death of the Dagenham cobbler. Sometime in 1606 'Christ[opher] Courts [&] George Radsdale' were presented 'For burying one Christ[ophe]r [blank]' a 'cobbler dwelling in the same parish [of Dagenham] at xii of the clocke at noone daye'. The burial in and of itself involved the sexton and does not immediately warrant any breach of common practice. 'That he [the Cobbler] was alive at viij of the Clocke on the morning of the same daie', however, points to an undue haste that is born out by the fact that this burial took place 'without touching of any bell or anie dutie done by the minister'. The matter appeared to take a more sinister turn as 'the said Christr had certayne money at the same tyme to the value of vli and certayne wares in his shoppe wch they [Courts and Radsdale] . . . sould, and distributed between them'. Here the lack of the bell tolling appeared to mask the alleged theft of money and goods. Yet the events were more complicated than the base reason of theft. Courts and Radsdale reported that 'the said p[a]rtie [the cobbler] was found dead in the highway and that there upon they both thought he dyed of the plague'. The fear of plague, which was a highly emotional response to a life-threatening reality, was one situation that precluded the usual Protestant emotional responses of providing suitable bell-ringing and a burial by a minister, in favour of a hasty burial. In an act aimed at preserving their emotional community and themselves 'there uppon thee both did helpe to carry to Church and that the Sexton did bury him'. The breach of the usual emotional communities response resulted in a rumour, that was only quashed when the events were investigated, and it was revealed that 'they recd noe p[a]rte of his goods'. Communal emotions, such as fear, explain the absence of tolling bell sounds, as in this case of the hasty burial of a plague victim. In his diary, the Reverend Ralph Josselin of Earls Colne, Essex in 1644 recounted that 'the plague continued and increased at (Col)chester, our town yet in safety Lord keep that destroying arrow from among us' (Macfarlane, *Earls*

---

1 Essex Record Office, D/AEA.24, vol. IV, folio 3, A.D. 1606, page 125 recto & verso.

38   *Dolly MacKinnon*

Colne, Essex: Records of an English Village, 1375–1854, Diary of Ralph Josselin (Private Collection), 26.8.1644).[2] In 1665, Josselin noted 'God good in our preservation, yet much endangered by Colchester. a lad of our parish coming then died in White Colne, feared of the infection, another among us of his company(,) lord preserve us. the weather sad, but this day cooling, died at London plague 4237. all. 5568. god in mercy stop infection. the increase was small in comparison of what feared. god good in the word, make it lord a soul blessing.'[3] Fear had altered the early modern soundscape of death, and in this instance of plague the bells fell silent. Yet the bells as an auditory marker of the excess of plague deaths was unmistakable in July 1665 during the Great Plague of London, when Samuel Pepys noted 'Sad news of deaths of so many in the parish of plague . . . The bell always going' (Gittings, 1984, p. 135).

Conclusion

The presence or absence of bell tolling in the two case studies I have discussed demonstrates the different responses to death by various emotional communities within early seventeenth-century England. In both instances those who did, as well as those who did not toll the bell, did so on the grounds of an emotional response to the Protestant communities' practices. Howard purposefully had the bells toll before and after his death in order to resonate a Roman Catholic religious practice now prohibited. The contravention of a Protestant emotional communities' mourning was proclaimed by the unceasing tolling of that bell for 48 hours throughout the London landscape. While at the other end of the social scale, in the case of the Dagenham cobbler in Essex who in 1606 was buried within four hours of his death, his fellow parishioners and neighbours complained and abhorred that his death and funeral had occurred 'without any tolling of a bell'. His hasty burial had resulted in this omission, and the communal fear of the plague had overturned this Protestant communal expectation of a tolling bell. Some parishioners considered that the bell should have tolled by right, as the bell sounded not simply as a reflection of his social status, but also as a call to prayer for others that marked his place in an emotional community of Dagenham in Essex in 1606. The absence of a Protestant communal form of a death knell in the parish of Dagenham challenged this parish's practice in Essex. Through my discussion of the two case-studies of the death of Henry Howard in 1614, and an Essex Cobbler in 1606, I have demonstrated that bells tolling for the dead both united and divided parish communities along the fault lines of the rituals of death, burial and mourning.

2 Macfarlane, Alan (eds), *Earls Colne, Essex: Records of an English Village, 1375–1854, Diary of Ralph Josselin (Private Collection),* 26.8.1644 (Monday 26 August 1644), document 70000110 (http://linux02.lib.cam.ac.uk/earlscolne/diary/70000110.htm) (Accessed 20 August 2014).

3 Macfarlane, Alan (eds), *Earls Colne, Essex: Records of an English Village, 1375–1854,* Diary of Ralph Josselin (Private Collection) 27.8.1665 (Sunday 27 August 1665) document 70014860, (http://linux02.lib.cam.ac.uk/earlscolne/diary/70000110.htm) (Accessed 20 August 2014).

References

Attali, J. (1985). *Noise: The Political Economy of Music* [*Bruits: essai sur l'économie politique de la musique*], tr. Brian Massumi. Manchester: Manchester University Press. [Paris: Universitaires de France, 1977]

Bourne, H. (1725). *Antiquities Vulgares; or, the Antiquities of the Common People. Giving account of Several of their opinions and ceremonies with Proper reflections upon each of them; shewing which may be retain'd and which ought to be laid aside.* Newcastle: J. White.

Chidley, S. (1656). *To His Highness the Lord Protector, &c. and to the Parliament of England. Valiant Swordmen, and Honorable Gentlemen.* London: [no publisher details listed].

Cressy, D. (1989). *Bonfires and Bells: National Memory and the Protestant Calendar in Elizabethan and Stuart England.* London: Weidenfeld and Nicholson.

Cressy, D. (1999). *Birth, marriage, and death: ritual, religion, and the Life-Cycle in Tudor and Stuart England.* Oxford: Oxford University Press, 1997.

Essex Record Office, D/AEA.24, vol. IV, folio 3, A.D. 1606.

Garrioch, D. (2003). Sounds of the City: the soundscapes of early modern European towns. *Urban History, 30*(1), 5–25.

Gittings, C. (1984). *Death, burial and the individual in Early Modern Britain.* London: Croom Helm.

Macfarlane, Alan (eds). *Earls Colne, Essex: Records of an English Village, 1375–1854.* (http://linux02.lib.cam.ac.uk/). (Accessed 20 August 2014).

MacKinnon, D. (2007). Hearing the English Reformation: Earls Colne, Essex. In R. Bandt, M. Duffy & D. MacKinnon (Eds.), *Hearing Places: Sound, Place, Time and Culture* (pp. 255–267). Newcastle, England: Cambridge Scholars Publishing.

MacKinnon, D. (2014). *Earls Colne's Early Modern Landscapes.* Aldershot: Ashgate.

Marsh, C. (2010). *Music and Society in Early Modern England.* Cambridge: Cambridge University Press.

McClure, N. E. (ed.) (1939). *The letters of John Chamberlain* (2 volumes). Memoirs XII, Part I, The American Philosophical Society. Philadelphia: The Lancaster Press.

Postles, D. (2006). 'Ringing out those bells': Death and the Social Order in early-modern Leicestershire. *Transactions of the Leicestershire Archaeological and Historical Society, 80*, 31–41.

Rosenwein, B. H. (2006). *Emotional communities in the early Middle Ages.* Ithaca, New York: Cornell University Press.

Schafer, R. M. (1977). *The Tuning of the World.* New York: Knopf.

Scholefield, J. (ed.) (1842). *The Works of James Pilkington.* Cambridge: Parker Society.

Smith, B. R. (1999). *The Acoustic World of Early Modern England.* Chicago: University of Chicago Press.

Truax, B. (1984). *Acoustic Communication.* New Jersey: Ablex Publishing Corporation.

Woodward, J. (1997). *Theatre of Death: The Ritual Management of Royal Funerals in Renaissance England.* Woodbridge: The Boydell Press.

5 Haunting Music
Hearing the Voices of the Dead

Helen Dell

Introduction

In bereavement many are 'haunted' by their dead – it seems to be an aspect of their mourning.[1] A. Grimby (1993) found that around 82% of elderly participants in his study experienced hallucinations or visions in the month following the death of their loved one, while 30% reported hearing their voice. Tales of the returning dead can also be found in that branch of the popular ballads known as revenant ballads. Within a psychoanalytic framework based on Sigmund Freud's theories of mourning in 'Totem and taboo' and 'Mourning and melancholia' I consider these questions: when the dead return what do they tell the living? Or rather, what do we hear because we long or dread to hear it? What can these haunting voices tell us of mourning, the struggle of the bereaved with the incomprehensible disappearance of the dead and their own appalling loss?

In modern popular culture the dead return with diametrically opposed sentiments towards the living. On one side they return as friendly spirits to assure the bereaved of their continuing love and care for them; on the other, they return as vengeful ghosts, vampires, zombies or demons, full of hatred and envy, to harm the living. I propose that these contradictory attitudes which the living attribute to the dead reflect the ambivalent feelings of the bereaved themselves towards their lost loved-ones. Freud's theories offer an understanding of the conflict between the socially acceptable and unacceptable aspects of mourning, which in contrasting expressions of popular culture are projected onto the dead.

The chapter begins by outlining some recent expressions of these opposing views of the intentions of the dead towards the living. I draw attention to them because, in my reading, they indicate that, although fewer people now give credence to the existence of the returning dead, the persistence of such cultural phenomena nonetheless indicates a continuing fascination with such beings.

The following section is devoted to a reading of two revenant ballads (those in which the dead return to converse with the living) in the light of these psychoanalytic ideas of mourning. In both ballads the dead return to confront

---

1 Darian Leader, in *The New Black: Mourning, Melancholia and Depression*, and Laurence A. Rickels, in *Aberrations of Mourning*, have both written on mourning from a psychoanalytic perspective. In their books they discuss various kinds of 'haunting'.

Haunting Music 41

their murderers. In Freud's account in 'Mourning and melancholia' certain mourners take responsibility for the deaths of their loved-ones:

> Where there is a disposition to obsessional neurosis the conflict due to ambivalence gives a pathological cast to mourning and forces it to express itself in the form of self-reproaches to the effect that the mourner himself is to blame for the loss of the loved object, i.e. that he has willed it. (Freud, 1991, p. 260)

If this is the case, the dead may return as spirits seeking justice or vengeance rather than as friendly guides and protectors. Both ballads recount family murders, one involving two sisters, the other a mother and her newborn babies. The breaking of these earliest and deepest of bonds, especially that between a mother and her children, communicates well Freud's idea that for those closest to the recently deceased the death is in some sense a murder for which they are responsible. In my reading these two murder/revenant ballads demonstrate that ambivalence of mourning to which Freud refers.[2]

The final section of the chapter addresses the question of how the ballads work on the listener beyond the message conveyed by the words, through their poetic and musical form. Here psychoanalytic theory since Freud is important, particularly when joined to semiotic theories based on the work of Ferdinand Saussure. Those of Julia Kristeva and Jacques Lacan address those aspects of speech which are surplus to communication. The popular ballads, in their formal arrangement of the material, in particular musical and textual repetition, offer the listener something not contained within the narrative.

Friendly Ghosts and the Vengeful Dead

A 2012 study by Katherine Keen *et al.* notes that, while many bereaved people maintain a continuing relation with their dead,

> an aspect of this continued relationship that has been relatively underresearched is the compelling experience of continuing to sense the presence of the deceased. This may involve the perception of being able to see, hear, feel the touch of, and converse with the deceased person, so that they are on occasions still present and available to them in some manner which contradicts the knowledge that the bereaved person has of that person's corporeal death. (Keen *et al.*, 2013, p. 384)

The internet abounds with uplifting stories of friendly visitations by the dead, unmediated by professional mediums, the so-called ADCs, that is, After Death Communications. These websites offer to the bereaved the kinds of consolation previously provided by traditional Spiritualism now made globally accessible by the new

---

2 Although there are numerous revenant ballads and even more murder ballads there are few that combine the two.

42   *Helen Dell*

technology. An ADC is, in the words of Edie Devers and Katherine Morton Robinson, an experience of the deceased 'through one or more of the five senses, through vivid dreams, or [through sensing] the presence of the deceased' (2002, p. 245). These are some messages offered as typical examples on the TRU paranormal website:

> I'm okay . . . I'm fine . . . Everything is okay . . . Don't worry about me . . .
>
> Don't grieve for me . . . Please let me go . . . I'm happy . . . Everything will be all right . . .
>
> Go on with your life . . . Please forgive . . . Thank you . . . I'll always be there for you . . .
>
> I'm watching over you . . . I'll see you again . . . I love you . . . Good-bye . . . (TRU paranormal Facebook page)[3]

These are the messages the grieving long to hear: death is not final, the dead exist on another plane; they are happy; they love us; they are watching over us and will meet us again. This aspect of after death communication is heavily stressed:

> According to our research, the purpose of these visits and signs by those who have died is to offer comfort, reassurance, and hope to their parents, spouse, siblings, children . . . They want you to know they're still alive and that you'll be reunited with them when it's your time to leave this physical life on earth – and they'll be there to greet you when you make your transition . . . *Nearly* all ADCs are positive, joyful, and uplifting encounters that reduce grief, provide lasting comfort and hope, and accelerate emotional and spiritual healing. (TRU paranormal, my emphasis)

There is a clear intention here on the part of the website creator (unnamed) to provide such experiences as a source of comfort, reassurance and hope to the bereaved despite the admission that not quite all do so. But by their pointed omission these messages implicitly draw attention to other, less consoling experiences of the bereaved: experiences of guilt, rage, ambivalence, self-reproach – all the more complicated and uncomfortable aspects of mourning. These unspoken pains of bereavement are, I believe, the very ones for which the ADC websites attempt to offer consolation. It is demonstrated by their emphatic assurance that the dead are, almost universally, well-intentioned towards their bereaved.[4]

---

3 Similarly uplifting messages from the dead can be found on a range of websites, for instance 'The after death communication research foundation' created by Judy and Jeffrey Long, and the after-death.com website created by Bill and Judy Guggenheim. There are also numerous books written in the same edifying tone by professional mediums, for instance: Concetta Bertoldi's *Inside the Other Side*, Patrick Mathews' *Forever with You*, Carole J. Obley's *I'm still with You* and Faye Schindelker's *Poppies from Heaven*.

4 Edie Devers in her PhD dissertation related some of the more difficult aspects of after death communication: 'Most times the communication was of a neutral or pleasant nature, many times helping

One does not have to look far to find what is omitted in these consoling messages. The other side of the coin is well represented in endless stories and images of the malicious and vengeful dead or undead: ghosts, vampires, zombies and demons. Here the dead are not the happy souls described in ADC messages. Nor do they love the living. They seek to harm and destroy them. In many communities the malice of the dead has been kept at bay only by the most stringent rituals such as those Freud describes in 'Totem and Taboo' (1990, pp. 107–113). Freud cites Rudolf Kleinpaul (1845–1914), a German writer who held the view that 'originally [. . .] the dead were all vampires, who bore ill-will to the living, and strove to harm them and deprive them of life' (Freud, 1990, p. 115). In our more sceptical age, even if we no longer retain a rational belief in such beings, they still haunt us via the horror genre in film, television and literature. They have not disappeared from our imaginations.[5]

The Revenant Ballads: Murder and Mourning

The same is true of the popular ballads, narrative songs addressing some of the most profound aspects of human life: love and hatred, jealousy, loss, betrayal and death. The oldest can be traced back to the Middle Ages. 'Judas' (Child, 1965, v.1. 23, p. 242) dates from a thirteenth-century manuscript (p. 242). They have a long and complicated history, in the oral tradition and in print, and have served different purposes at different times (for instance as a means of social control) but now, when their usefulness for such purposes has diminished, the ballads are still being sung. For instance, Anna Helle, a Finnish scholar currently researching the continuation of the ballad tradition in modern popular song, writes of the vitality of the murder ballad tradition, citing Nick Cave and the Bad Seeds' *Murder Ballads* album of 1996.[6] These songs of murder and betrayal still move the listener. It is with such continuities that I am concerned here rather than with the passing inflections of particular historical moments.[7]

---

the participants resolve their grief. Sometimes, however, the communication was difficult. Some participants had unresolved issues or conflicted relationships with the deceased. Like people resolving issues in any relationship, those who have experienced the deceased may need help in resolving the conflicts, or may want someone to listen' (Devers: 1994, p. 118).

5 Author and psychoanalyst Lou Andreas-Salomé (1861–1937) an associate of Freud's, reflected that 'film technique alone approximates, through its rapid alternation of images, our own powers of imagination' (cited in Rickels 2011, p. 147). A sample of horror films on the hostile dead theme includes the 1961 *The Pit and the Pendulum* (1961), directed by Roger Corman, based on Edgar Allen Poe's story of the same name, *The Fog* (1980) and *The Ward* (2010), both directed by John Carpenter, *The St. Francisville Experiment* (2000), dir. Ted Nicolaou and *Left for Dead*, a 2007 horror Western dir. Albert Pyun.

6 Helle mentions other instances: 'Bob Dylan ("Lily of the West"), Nirvana ("In the Pines"/"Where did you sleep last night"), and Johnny Cash ("I hung my head"), only to give a few examples. Thus, although the genre may at the first sight appear a leftover from ancient times, it is strikingly lively and popular today' (Helle, 2014, unpublished abstract, p. 1).

7 David Atkinson covers some historical aspects of 'The Cruel Mother', in 'History, Symbol and Meaning' pp. 360–362.

44 *Helen Dell*

Example 5.1 'The Twa Sisters' (Binnorie), musical transcription, anon., as sung by Custer LaRue

When the dead speak to the living in traditional English and Scottish revenant ballads (a revenant is simply one who returns after death in some shape or form) they rarely bring messages of consolation. In the revenant ballads the dead speak with authority. Their pronouncements have the status of truth, even prophecy. In these ballads the dead know more than the living; death apparently gives them a better vantage point, and, in the case of the murdered dead, they seem compelled to return and impart their knowledge, to pass judgement or to seek revenge on the living.

This is the case in 'The Twa Sisters' ('Binnorie') where the dead woman returns to point the finger at the sister who murdered her for jealousy (Child, v. I: 10, 118).[8] For this and the following ballad I have chosen, from recordings easily available to the reader, those with simple accompaniments and an unaffected style of singing. They are on the whole not over-dramatised, allowing the ballads to work via their own unique blend of narrative, melody and form.

There were twa sisters sat in a bow'r
Binnorie O Binnorie
There cam a knight to be her wooer
By the bonny mill dams of Binnorie

He courted the elder wi' glove and ring
But he lo'ed the youngest aboon a' thing.

The eldest she was vexéd sair
And sore envied her sister fair.

The eldest said to the youngest ane:
'Will you go and see our father's ships come in.'

She's ta'en her by the lily hand,
And led her down the river strand.

The youngest stude upon a stane,
The eldest cam' and pushed her in.

---

8 'The Twa Sisters' ('Binnorie') is sung by Custer LaRue on *Daemon Lover: The Traditional Ballads and Songs of England, Scotland and America.*

'O sister, sister, reach your hand,
And ye shall be heir of all my land.'

'O sister, I'll not reach my hand,
And I'll be heir of all your land.'

'O sister, reach me but your glove,
And sweet William shall be your love.'

'Sink on, nor hope for hand nor glove,
And sweet William had better be my love.'

Sometimes she sank, sometimes she swam,
Until she cam to the miller's dam.

The miller's daughter was baking bread,
And gaed for water as she had need.

'O father, father, draw your dam!
There's either a mermaid or a milk-white swan.'

The miller hasted and drew his dam,
And there he found a drown'd woman.

Ye couldna see her yellow hair
For gowd and pearls that were sae rare.

You couldna see her middle sma',
Her gowden girdle was sae braw.

Ye couldna see her lily feet,
Her gowden fringes were sae deep.

A famous harper passing by,
That sweet pale face did chance to spy.

And when he looked that lady on,
He sighed and made a heavy moan.

He made a harp o' her breast bone,
Whose sounds would melt a heart of stone.

The strings he framed of her yellow hair
Their sounds made sad the listening ear.

He's ta'en it to her father's ha',
There were the court assembled a'.

He laid the harp upon a stane,
And straight it began to play alane –

'And yonder sits my father, the king
And yonder sits my mother the queen.

And yonder stands my brother Hugh,
And beside him my William, sweet and true.'

But the last tune that the harp played then
Was – 'Woe to my sister, false Helen!'

Example 5.2 'The Twa Sisters' (Binnorie), text transcription, anon., as sung by Custer
LaRue (from CD liner notes)

46 *Helen Dell*

Example 5.3 'The Cruel Mother', musical transcription, anon., as sung by Shirley Collins.

In the ballad two sisters love the same man. He openly courts the elder but loves the (more beautiful) younger sister 'aboon a' thing'. The elder sister lures the younger to her death by drowning. A musician then discovers her dead body and makes it into an instrument which, when played before her family, accuses her sister of the murder and sometimes insists on her execution.

'The Cruel Mother' (Child, v. I: 20, p. 218),[9] speaks of that instance of family murder which most haunts me, infanticide – the illicit love, the mother's lonely pregnancy and birth which must be hidden from everyone, the murder, the haunting voices of the children, the judgement.[10]

>A minister's daughter in the north
>– *Hey the rose and the lindsay-o,*
>She's fallen in love with her father's clerk,
>   – *Down by the greenwood side-i-o.*
>
>He courted her for a year and a day,
>Till her the young man did betray.
>
>She leaned her back up against a tree
>And there the tear did blind her eye.
>
>She leaned her back up against a thorn
>And there her bonny boys she has born.
>
>She's taken out her little pen-knife
>And she has twined them of their life.
>
>She laid them beneath some marble stone
>Thinking to go a maiden home.
>
>As she looked over her father's wall
>She saw her two bonny boys playing ball.
>
>'Oh bonny boys, if you were mine
>I'd dress you up in silk so fine.'

9 Shirley Collins sings 'The Cruel Mother' on the album *The Sweet Primroses*. She was taught this variant by Ewan McColl, who learnt it from his mother, Betty Miller.
10 Ingrid Lana Scher notes the haunting presence of the murderous mother in cultural narrative: 'If, as author Toni Morrison believes, we tell stories about what we find most terrifying, then our cultural narratives suggest an overwhelming preoccupation with the murderous mother – the monster in our minds' (Scher, 2005, Abstract).

'Oh cruel mother, when we were thine
We didn't see aught of your silk so fine.'

'Oh bonny boys, come tell to me
What sort of death I shall have to die?'

'Seven years as a fish in the flood,
And seven years a bird in the wood.'

'Seven years a tongue in the warning bell,
And seven years in the flames of hell.'

'Welcome, welcome, fish in the flood,
And welcome, welcome, bird in the wood.'

'Welcome, tongue to the warning bell,
But God keep me from the flames of hell.'

Example 5.4 'The Cruel Mother', text transcription, anon., as sung by Shirley Collins

This song speaks to all parents, particularly mothers. Most of us do not liter-ally kill our children but we all know that we harm or neglect them at one time or another. There are many variants of 'The Cruel Mother' in Child's collection alone (see Child, v. I: 20, pp. 218–227). In fact no two singers will sing a ballad in exactly the same way, but in each an unmarried woman becomes pregnant and kills her newborn child or children to hide her shame. The children later appear to her and accuse her of her crime, usually outlining the punishments she will undergo after death.

In 'Totem and Taboo' (1913) Freud attempted to analyse the terror which the dead may inspire in the living. He drew on the work of his contemporaries, includ-ing Finnish social anthropologist, philosopher and sociologist, Edvard Alexander Westermarck, from whom he quoted in this passage:

The hypothesis that after their death those most beloved were transformed into demons clearly raises further questions. What was it that induced primi-tive men to attribute such a change of feeling to those who had been dear to them? Why did they make them into demons? Westermarck . . . is of the opinion that these questions can be answered easily. 'Death is commonly regarded as the gravest of all misfortunes; hence the dead are believed to be exceedingly dissatisfied with their fate. According to primitive ideas a person only dies if he is killed – by magic if not by force – and such a death naturally tends to make the soul revengeful and ill-tempered. It is envious of the living and is longing for the company of its old friends; no wonder, then, that it sends them diseases to cause their death . . . But the notion that the disembodied soul is on the whole a malicious being . . . is also, no doubt, intimately connected with the instinctive fear of the dead, which is in its turn the outcome of the fear of death.' (Freud, 1990, p. 115)

Freud offered his own psychoanalytic reading of this fear. He spoke of the 'tormenting scruples' which afflict the bereaved who reproach themselves

48   *Helen Dell*

with guilt for the death of their loved ones through carelessness or neglect and cannot be consoled. Freud asserts that such reproaches are, in one sense, justified:

> It is not that the mourner was really responsible for the death . . . Nonetheless there was something in her − a wish that was unconscious to herself − which would not have been dissatisfied by the occurrence of death and which might actually have brought it about if it had had the power. And after death *has* occurred, it is against this unconscious wish that the reproaches are a reaction. In almost every case where there is an intense emotional attachment to a particular person we find that behind the tender love there is a concealed hostility in the unconscious. (Freud, 1990, p. 116)

For Freud, as for Westermarck, the death of a loved one may, in a sense, be considered a murder. Freud drew a distinction between those societies which, speaking the language of his time and place, he called primitive, and the neurotic patients he saw in his consulting room. For 'primitive' people, Freud believed, unconscious hostility is displaced onto the dead, whereas for his patients, it is taken on as guilt for an imagined failure in care for the deceased. Both these displacements, however, stemmed from the impossibility of reconciling the ambivalent emotions of the bereaved towards their dead, the conscious grief and the hidden satisfaction (Freud, 1990, p. 117).

Freud returned to the theme of self-reproach a few years later, in 'Mourning and Melancholia' (1917). 'Melancholia' is an older term which these days is usually subsumed in psychiatric discourse under the catch-all phrase 'depression'.[11] Freud distinguished melancholia from mourning in this way:

> The distinguishing mental features of melancholia are a profoundly painful dejection, cessation of interest in the outside world, loss of the capacity to love, inhibition of all activity, and a lowering of the self-regarding feelings to a degree that finds utterance in self-reproaches and self-revilings, and culminates in a delusional expectation of punishment. (Freud 1991, p. 254)[12]

It is that self-reproach that distinguishes the melancholic for Freud (although elsewhere in 'Mourning and Melancholia' he has related it to the obsessional). It comes about, he wrote, in this way:

---

11 From a psychoanalytic point of view depression is an inadequate term. Darian Leader considers it mechanistic and superficial, useful only to describe 'a set of symptoms that derive from complex and always different human stories' (2008, p. 3).

12 Some of these symptoms may be found, differently expressed, under the term complicated grief. See, for instance, these symptoms in the Horowitz *et al.* 1997 study: 'emotionally numb to others', 'regrets own actions towards the deceased' and 'feeling worthless' (Table 1, p. 906).

Haunting Music 49

[T]he shadow of the [lost] object fell upon the ego, and the latter could hence-
forth be judged by a special agency, as though it were an object, the forsaken
object. In this way an object-loss was transformed into an ego-loss and the
conflict between the ego and the loved person [transformed] into a cleavage
between the critical activity of the ego and the ego as altered by identification.
(Freud, 1991, p. 258)

In this way the bereaved prescribes his or her own penance for the 'murder' of
the one who has died. What I am suggesting is that the judgement of the dead
in these two murder ballads could be construed as that self-reproach which the
melancholic heaps on him or herself in the way Freud describes: that is, that
the ego is split, one half becoming an object that is judged by the other, and,
in the case of these songs, judgement is projected as the voice of the dead.
But I wonder whether this self-reproach is not, in varying degrees, present
in all mourning – whether we do not all say at some time: 'if only I had been
there, if only I had not failed her in that crucial moment'. The greatest part of
the anguish stems from the knowledge that it can never be put right. The time
for reparation is past, which is why people seek the reassurance that forms of
Spiritualism like the ADC websites offer. Freud's other distinction, between
'primitive' societies and modern neurotics, also looks a little shaky in the light
of these songs. Unless we wish to label the murder ballads primitive, along
with the endless procession of vampire and zombie films of the present day,
modern humanity does not seem to have outgrown the projection of unconscious hostility onto the dead.

There is another aspect to the judgements the dead make on the living. We
can, of course, also hear in these murder ballads the voices of living judges, the
law, the church, the helping professions, all those who have a say in how we
behave, and who try to set the world to rights after an appalling event, wanting
to put everything and everyone back in their proper places, the guilty identified
and punished, order restored. We hear, perhaps in folk song especially, what
matters to communities at a given time and place. But I have chosen to write
here, in the singular, of the haunted – those who tread the lonely and desolate
path of mourning.

The Ballads as Song

So far I have not mentioned the difference music makes to the messages of the
dead. I think that what we hear the dead sing to us matters greatly. One website I
have looked at suggests:

Music seems to be a favourite means of afterlife communication used by
the deceased. It seems that music is manipulated fairly easily by those
experiencing life after death, perhaps due to its vibratory nature and
unique frequency. Many who are grieving the death of a loved one have

50   *Helen Dell*

> relayed experiences to me of hearing songs that are highly relevant to the
> deceased, playing at extremely unlikely yet opportune moments. (wisdom-
> of-spirit.com)

I would say, rather, that we are most haunted by song because of the power of
music (and poetry) to affect us deeply.

There are many ways in which to describe the affective power of music. I
have turned to the discourse of French semiotic and psychoanalytic theory for
assistance in finding the words for what is difficult to say of that power. Freud
was not concerned with music. He proclaimed himself 'ganz unmusikalisch'
(completely unmusical). Nor was he familiar with the developments in linguistic
theory, unpublished in his time, which found a response and a reaction in the work
of Julia Kristeva, Jacques Lacan and Roland Barthes, around the end of the 1960s
and through the 1970s. These developments, by focusing attention on the formal,
non-communicative aspects of song, cast a different light on the power that music
has to haunt us and thus, indirectly, on the sufferings of mourning.

Kristeva, in *Revolution in poetic language*, pointed out that poetry and song
emphasise the non-communicative, 'genotextual' aspects of speech, 'phonematic
devices (such as the accumulation and repetition of phonemes or rhyme) and
melodic devices (such as intonation or rhythm)' (Kristeva, 1984, p. 86). These
are the characteristics that emerge in listening. Kristeva opposes genotext to phenotext, that is, 'language that serves to communicate' (p. 87). The phenotext is
the language described by phonology, that is, 'language [in which] there are only
differences [. . .] without positive terms' (Ferdinand de Saussure, 1974, p. 120).
It is language to which the materiality of sound is surplus, language reduced to the
bone of signification—the 'message'. Communication deplores confusion and the
genotextual aspects of speech which Kristeva termed 'semiotic' threaten signify-
ing unity. But songs, as sound and form, cannot be reduced to the message they
convey although they are often spoken of as if they can.

Lacan too spoke of a form of utterance he named *lalangue*, which, he said,
'serves purposes that are altogether different from that of communication' (Lacan,
1999, p. 138). He added:

> That is what the experience of the unconscious has shown us, insofar as it is
> made of *lalangue*, which, as you know I write with two l's to designate what
> each of us deals with, our so-called mother tongue . . . which isn't called that
> by accident. (p. 138)

I think that one sense of *lalangue* is that joy in sound that we hear in the
meaningless dialogues between mother and infant, and which persists through
life as song. From the perspective of meaningful communication *lalangue* is
flawed. It delights in confusion, as Lacan delighted in demonstrating with an
endless stream of homophones, like 'tu es', you are, and 'tuer', to kill. Both
Lacan and Kristeva were psychoanalysts who listened to the slips and the
confused babbling of their analysands. They listened, not only for meanings

but for what must be ignored in language when meaning is the only issue – *lalangue* (Lacan, 1999, 139).

Roland Barthes adapted Kristeva's argument to speak of vocal music in particular. He felt the need to attempt 'the impossible account of an individual thrill that [he] constantly experience[d] in listening to singing' (Barthes, 1977, p. 181). In Barthes' essay, Kristeva's phenotext became pheno-song, her genotext geno-song. Of the pheno-song, exemplified in the essay by the singing of Dietrich Fischer-Dieskau, he said:

> The pheno-song covers all the phenomena, all the features which belong to the structure of the language being sung, the rules of the genre, the coded form of the melisma, the composer's idiolect, the style of the interpretation: in short, everything in the performance which is in the service of communication, representation, expression. (Barthes, 1977, p. 182)

The geno-song, exemplified for Barthes by the Russian church bass and by the baritone Charles Panzera, is not in the service of communication. It is 'the grain', 'the materiality of the body speaking its mother tongue' (p. 182). It is

> that apex (or that depth) of production where the melody really works at the language – not at what it says, but the voluptuousness of its sounds-signifiers, of its letters – where melody explores how the language works and identifies with that work. (p. 182)

I do not entirely agree with Barthes' conclusions. I am not convinced (especially when I listen to Panzera) that one cannot have both the pheno- and the geno-song – both soul and body in Barthes' terms (pp. 181–183). In fact I think one must, because both come in the one package. But for my purposes here, the work of these three theorists gestures towards what, in a song, goes beyond communication, representation or expression. These three terms assume that there is something *behind* the song to be communicated, represented and expressed – an essential message which a good interpretation will extract. I wish to speak also of what cannot be extracted – something which *represents* nothing, something in the very grain of the song. One cannot take it apart if its power is to be, not precisely understood, but experienced and honoured.

We cannot, in the case of folk song – where melodies and texts change partners all the time – say much of particular text–music relationships, but we can speak generally of the effect the genotextual qualities of song produce to reach beyond the simple meaning of the words. Certain musical effects will create an emphasis on any text they encounter, for instance the modal shift from Ionian to Mixolydian on the first note of the last line of 'The Cruel Mother'. It may be pure coincidence that the drop from d sharp to d natural occurs on the word 'down' in the second refrain of each strophe, but it certainly darkens the atmosphere of the song. Music and words together have an energy, an intensity, a memorability, which neither could produce without the other. The singing voice alone, in its particularity, has

52   Helen Dell

a power for which no explanation is sufficient. The listener's experience will always exceed explanation because song speaks also from that inexhaustible well of possibility, the heterogenous *lalangue*, and in doing so exceeds anything that can be said of it.

Bertrand Harris Bronson, who reunited the Child ballads with their missing 'musical half', insisted that ballad texts and music could only be studied together, and lamented that for so long they had been studied apart:

> And before any other approach was thinkable an unnatural divorce had to be effected between two elements [text and melody] which had always existed, not side by side, but so inextricably interwoven that even Psyche's 'confused seeds' were not more intermixed. (Bronson, 1969, p. 37)

Of Kristeva's components of genotext, 'phonematic devices (. . . accumulation and repetition of phonemes or rhyme) and melodic devices (such as intonation or rhythm)' (1984, p. 86), repetition of various kinds is the one which strikes the ear first in any popular ballad. What Kristeva does not say is that, in a strophic song (as opposed to through-composed), melody and rhythm are also repeated. Ballads are densely patterned by repetitions at every level.

The two murder ballads in the variants I have chosen are both, like most ballads, quatrains. These two have refrains on the second and fourth lines of each strophe leaving lines one and three to carry the narrative. The song rocks continually between forward movement and return. Thus the narrative proceeds very slowly, with these elements of rest interrupting it for half of every strophe. And the ballads are often quite long. Communication of the story (the phenotext) is, as Bronson noted, not dominant:

> Narrative . . . does not by its own nature consent . . . to be submissive to constant interruption and repetition at fixed points throughout its length, at the behest of an arbitrary and relatively uncompromising vehicle imposed to contain it by a power owning another lordship. (Bronson, 1976, p. xxiv)

If the message (the narrative) were the only point, these non-narrative elements would have been long banished. In the ballads the message must contend, or perhaps dance, with what resounds through the song – melodic and textual repetition. Ballad refrains communicate little. They are often meaningless in themselves; some are nonsense syllables like 'Fal the dal the dido'. Such refrains speak pure *lalangue*, indulging the sheer joy of sound, rhythm and rhyme. But some of these fragments resonate with the narrative in different ways. In many variants of 'The Cruel Mother', for instance, the first and second refrains, taken together, place a cumulative pressure on the sore point of the song – the lonely birth and murder. This occurs, for instance in Group A, 6 in Bronson: 'It was all alone and alon-e; Down by the greenwood si-de' (1976, p. 78). The value of such lines is purely affective. They sing from a point outside the narrative movement of the ballad, returning again and again, text and music interlaced, to the lonely woman and her babies in that lonely scene, never allowing the listener to forget. I think they can be heard as repeated lines of melancholic self-reproach. Shirley Collins, who sang this ballad, said something similar, that for her 'the refrain has the quality of an incantation, raising one wretched human being to an archetype of remorse' (Mainly Norfolk). An incantation is a spell, which is a good word for the affective power of the ballads.

There is another kind of repetition which folklorists call incremental – repetition with alteration. Usually the alteration occurs between strophes, ensuring that the altered line shares its music with its unaltered counterpart in the previous strophe, for instance here in 'The Cruel Mother' where the babies' ghosts confront their mother, Group C, 45 in Bronson. (refrain lines removed):

'Oh babes, oh babes if you were mine'
'I would dress you up in silks so fine'

'Oh mother dear when we were thine'
'You did not dress us up in silks so fine'

Here the altered text in the second strophe distinguishes itself from the repetition of the melody. But sometimes the melodic difference between the first and third narrative lines of each strophe serves to highlight the textual alteration, as in a broadside variant of 'The Two Sisters' (refrains removed):

Then bespake the treble string,
'O yonder is my father the king.'

Then bespake the second string,
'O yonder sitts my mother the queen.'

And then bespake the strings all three,
'O yonder is my sister that drowned mee.' (Child, v. 1, A.a, p. 126).

As in the first example, dialogue is often the stage for effects of contrast and confrontation. The effect is different in the second, leading up suddenly (though not unexpectedly) to the clinching line of accusation sung by the instrument made from the dead girl's body. In both cases, however, the power of the genotextual aspects of poetry and music to work on and with the narrative are evident. The patterns of repetition and difference woven through text and melody give a weight and an intensity to the stories which can only be fully experienced by the listener.

Many of the ballads are tragic; a number of them include death, often by murder (and, for the mourner, if he or she takes responsibility for it, any death is a kind of murder). These ballads offer a way to consider the pangs of mourning in music, firstly by what they say, but also by what is not explicitly said but which nevertheless speaks through them in poetic and musical form.

54   *Helen Dell*

References

After Death.com. http://web.archive.org/web/20071011195027/http://www.after-death. com/. (Accessed 8 August 2014).

Atkinson, D. (1992). History, Symbol, and Meaning in 'The Cruel Mother'. *Folk Music Journal, 6*(3), 359–380.

Barthes, R. (1977). The Grain of the Voice. *Image, Music, Text.* Selected and translated by S. Heath (pp. 179–189). New York: Hill and Wang.

Bronson, B. H. (1969). *The Ballad as Song.* Berkeley, CA: University of California Press.

Bronson, B. H. (1976). *The Singing Tradition of Child's Ballads.* Princeton, NJ: Princeton University Press.

Child, F. J., ed. (1965). *The English and Scottish Popular Ballads.* New York: Dover Publications.

Collins, S. (1995). The Cruel Mother. *The Sweet Primroses.* Topic Records, TSCD 476 UK. Available at https://www.youtube.com/watch?v=WGnO_epxOhc. (Accessed 15 August 2014).

Devers, E. (1994). Experiencing the Deceased: Reconciling the Extraordinary. PhD diss. University of Florida.

Devers, E. & Robinson, K. M. (2002). The making of a grounded theory: after death communication. *Death Studies, 26*(3), 241–253.

Freud, S. (1990). Totem and Taboo. *The Origins of Religion.* Ed. and trans. James Strachey (pp. 43–224). London: Penguin.

Freud, S. (1991). Mourning and Melancholia. *On Metapsychology.* Ed. and trans. James Strachey (pp. 245–268). London: Penguin.

Grimby, A. (1998). Hallucinations following the loss of a spouse: Common and normal events among the elderly. *Journal of Clinical Geropsychology, 4*, 65–74.

Horowitz, M. J., B. Siegel, A. Holen, G. A. Bonanno, C. Milbrath, & C. H. Stinson. (1997). Diagnostic Criteria for Complicated Grief Disorder. *American Journal of Psychiatry, 154*(7), 904–910.

Keen, C., C. Murray, & S. Payne. (2013). Sensing the Presence of the Dead: A Narrative Review. *Mental Health, Religion and Culture, 16*(4), 384–402.

Kristeva, J. (1984). *Revolution in Poetic Language.* New York: Columbia University Press.

Lacan, J. (1999) *On Feminine Sexuality: The Limits of Love and Knowledge: Encore, 1972–1973.* Ed. J.-A. Miller. Trans. and notes B. Fink. New York: Norton.

LaRue, C. (1993). 'The Twa Sisters'. *Daemon Lover: The Traditional Ballads and Songs of England, Scotland and America.* Naxos: DOR-90174. Available at https://www.you tube.com/watch?v=SlB_QPMUWmg. (Accessed 21 July 2014).

Leader, D. (2008). *The New Black: Mourning, Melancholia and Depression.* London: Penguin.

Mainly Norfolk. 'The Cruel Mother/Greenwood Sidey/The Lady of York'. Available at http://mainlynorfolk.info/lloyd/songs/thecruelmother.html. (Accessed 20 August, 2014).

Rickels, L. A. (2011). *Aberrations of Mourning.* Minneapolis: University of Minnesota Press.

Saussure, F. de. (1974). *Course in General Linguistics.* Ed. C. Bally, A. Sechehaye, & A. Reidlinger. Trans. W. Baskin. Introd. J. Culler. Rev. ed. Glasgow: Fontana-Collins.

Scher, I. L. (2005). Monsters in our minds: the myth of infanticide and the murderous mother in the cultural psyche. PhD diss. University of New South Wales.

TRU paranormal Facebook: https://www.facebook.com/TRUPARANORMALINVESTI GATIONS/posts/602990099721610. (Accessed 24 July 2014).

Wisdom of Spirit Website. http://www.wisdom-of-spirit.com/afterlifecommunication. html. (Accessed 26 July 2014).

6 The Psychological Function of Music in Mourning Rituals

Examples from Three Continents

Sandra Garrido and Waldo F. Garrido

Introduction

Manifestations of grief vary in different cultures, between different individuals, and over time (Jalland, 2006). However, one key part of the grieving process in nearly all cultures is the use of rituals at various stages of the grieving process (Reeves & Boersma, 1989–1990). While there has been some increasing interest in the use of physical mementoes and their role in mourning, research into other ways people memorialise the deceased, such as with music, has thus far been limited (Doss, 2006; Woodthorpe, 2011). Music has been an important part of most rites of passage across cultures and time, including rituals surrounding death (Becker, 2001; Schechter, 1994). However, most of the research on music within the context of the funeral has taken place in the fields of historical musicology, ethnomusicology or anthropology, such as Steven Feld's profound work on the funerary weeping and song of the Kaluli of New Guinea (2012). There has been little research on music's function within the grieving process from a psychological perspective.

The anthropological literature reveals, however, that in many cultures specialised music within the funeral ritual allows the externalisation of feelings and a social medium in which grief can be acceptably expressed (Castle & Philips, 2003; Goss & Klass, 1997). This chapter therefore aims to explore the use of music in mourning rituals through the lens of some of the major theoretical approaches to bereavement. Rather than discussing the benefits or otherwise of the various approaches, we rather use them to illustrate the potential for music to play a key role in assisting with grief resolution. We use the term 'resolution' to refer to arriving at a state of reconciliation with the changed circumstances. We do not use it to refer to the disappearance of grief or to coming to the end of mourning. Rather, we have adopted the understanding of Silverman and Klass (1996), that grief resolution is the process of 'negotiating and renegotiating the meaning of the loss over time' (p. 19).

This chapter will look at the role of music by considering evidence from ethnographic and ethnomusicological studies into the use of music in mourning rituals in three specific cultural contexts with the hope that this will stimulate an interest in further empirical exploration of the issue in future research. In particular, we

56   Sandra Garrido and Waldo F. Garrido

will consider the jazz funeral from New Orleans in North America; from South America we will discuss the case of the 'cantos de ángeles' from Chile, a particular song form used for the funerals of very young children; and from Europe we will consider the role of the lament in Georgia. We will begin with a brief description of each ritual and its associated music before comparing and contrasting these rituals and examining them in the light of theories about coping with bereavement.

The Jazz Funeral

Grief may contain not only suffering, but also a sense of celebrating both the life of the deceased and the relationship with them (Castle & Philips, 2003). This was fairly common in many cultures until the twentieth century (Sakakeeny, 2011). One example of this is the jazz funeral found in Afro-American communities in regions of the United States. The jazz funeral originated in New Orleans, Louisiana, but similar customs are found amongst Afro-American communities in other parts of the country, such as Kentucky (Collins & Doolittle, 2006). The musicians participate in a wake prior to the funeral and also play hymns during the procession from the home to the church and then to the cemetery. However, at some point later the band begins to play more upbeat music, a moment known as 'turning or cutting the body loose' (Secundy, 1989, p. 101). Mourners may join the parade behind the marching musicians and dance as the procession moves to the burial site (Sakakeeny, 2011).

This spirit of celebration and rejoicing is basic to the jazz funeral and embodies the idea that through death the person has been liberated from the pain of life into a better condition (Secundy, 1989). Mourners thus often call the funeral a 'home-going celebration' (Collins & Doolittle, 2006, p. 959). It is also believed that a 'proper send-off' enables the deceased to cross over to the next life. Families with few resources may therefore spend a great deal of money on a lavish celebration to demonstrate how much the deceased was valued (Collins & Doolittle, 2006). The music is a pivotal part of expressing their belief in the hereafter and in creating an atmosphere of celebration.

Well-known melodies which are played in the parade, such as 'When the Saints Go Marching In', are intimately connected with the spiritual beliefs upholding these traditions. Afro-American funerals in other parts of the country will similarly often include upbeat music and singing where the choir and grievers clap and rock back and forth recalling the good deeds of the deceased (McIlwain, 2003), thus reassuring the bereaved of the deceased's place in heaven. It is not unusual for personalised choices of music, poetry or scripture to also be a part of the ceremony.

Although traditionally the jazz funeral was usually only for prominent Afro-American males, in recent years there has been a new trend in which jazz funerals are held for both men and women who have died tragically young (Sakakeeny, 2011). While the tradition declined in popularity during the 1970s, modern bands such as the Dirty Dozen Brass Band are reviving this tradition. Similar customs are now used in other regions of the US and have even been found in the UK thanks to a bands such as Jazz Not Jazz.

The Lament in Georgia

Belief in an afterlife is also central to the rituals surrounding death in Georgia. Georgia is situated at the dividing line between Asia and Europe. In Georgia, the lament is assigned the official function of softening the ground for the deceased to make her/his way into the hereafter (Kotthoff, 2001). As in the case of the Afro-American funeral customs discussed above, in Georgia it is believed that an appropriate send-off will ensure a good reception for the deceased in the hereafter. The mourning rituals are thus carefully choreographed in order to achieve this aim.

Laments are an interesting genre of music as they are found worldwide and in all historical periods and are an important part of a wake or vigil, a custom which itself has ancient origins (Schechter, 1994). One of the most distinctive and unique features of the Georgian lament is that it is polyphonic (containing several melodies sung at once) (Emsheimer, 1967). Traditionally, in some regions of Georgia, it was believed that the soul of the deceased found a temporary abode while this polyphonic lament was performed (Nakashidze, 2002). As in many non-Western cultures, individual expressions of emotion are subordinate to these rigorously prescribed public demonstrations (Wouters, 2002).

In most parts of Georgia, laments are performed by the women from the family and neighbourhood of the deceased, who gather around the coffin and, using the prescribed formats, eulogise the deceased, describing personal memories and addressing him or her directly (Kotthoff, 2006). Despite following strictly stylised forms, the laments are individually tailored to the deceased, containing personal memories and biographical details (Kotthoff, 2006).

As in many other parts of the world where lamentation is still practised, in Georgia laments are improvised, partly sung and partly spoken dialogues between lamenters (Kotthoff, 2001). The melody is often repetitive with sobbing sounds at the end of each line. The length and intensity of the lamenting expresses the social status of the deceased and how much they were valued by their family. A lament is considered 'good' if it provokes the listeners to tears, while those who do not mourn correctly can be seen as not having proper feelings of grief (Kotthoff, 2006).

'Cantos de ángeles' in Chile

As in the case of the jazz funeral, the concept of music and rejoicing in a funeral is also found in some parts of Latin America in the 'cantos de ángeles'. The 'cantos de ángeles' (songs of angels) is a particular song form used for the funerals of very young children (Dannemann, 2007), which originated in Spain and was brought to Latin America by Jesuit missionaries in the 1500s. In the nineteenth century variations of the ritual and the associated music could still be found

58 *Sandra Garrido and Waldo F. Garrido*

throughout much of Latin America and are widely used even in more recent times (Schechter, 1983).

While the funeral of an adult is unmistakably an occasion of mourning, sources from the nineteenth and early twentieth centuries indicate that wakes for 'angelitos' (little angels) in parts of Chile were wild parties with 'overtones of savagery and heresy' (Orellana, 1990). In fact, in one of the earliest references to the 'velorio de angelito' in Chile by Foster Coffin (cited in Schechter, 1994), the funeral was at first mistaken for the celebration of a saint's festival. More modern versions of 'cantos de ángeles' such as the one written by renowned popular music performer and folklorist Violetta Parra ('Rin Del Angelito') in 1964–1965 also depict the 'joyous atmosphere of a Chilean child's wake' (Schechter, 2009, p. 422). It is not uncommon for the celebrations to include the consumption of large amounts of alcohol, dancing and flirtatious behaviour.

The death of the child was an occasion of festivity since it was believed that a child who dies in a state of innocence becomes an angel (Schechter, 1994). In addition, it is believed that as an angel, the child will have divine grace and can become an intercessor for the family in heaven and a guide to his parents so that they themselves can reach heaven when the time comes (Orellana, 1990).

Rather than being placed in a coffin, in Chile the corpse of the child is dressed and made-up so as to appear as alive as possible and seated in a chair as if to witness its own funeral (Orellana, 1990). The child is dressed in a white 'tunica' or 'tunico' and wings are put upon it so that it looks like an angel. Singers known as 'cantores' are hired to sing the specialised verses (Orellana, 1990). These songs are used exclusively for infant funerals because of the superstition that if you sing the 'cantos de ángeles' without reason, a child will die (Orellana, 1990).

Although found throughout much of Latin America, the ritual has acquired special significance and unique features in parts of Chile such as the island of Chiloé, which remain largely unchanged to this day (Dannemann, 2007; Garrido & Garrido, 2011). The 'cantos', in particular, are an interesting example of the unique regional features the ritual has taken on. In Spain, for example, the singing of the 'cantos' takes place outside the house as an accompaniment to the funeral proceedings inside the house, while in Chile the singing occurs inside the house as an integral part of the ceremony and an essential element of the mourning (Orellana, 1990). In Spain it is believed that the child goes straight away to heaven upon death (Schechter, 1983). However, in Chile the singing of the 'cantos de ángeles' is considered to be a sort of magic ritual in which music and words are used to penetrate the spirit world and bring about the actual conversion of the deceased child to spirit life. It is thought that if a child's wake does not include the 'cantos de ángeles' the child is not able to leave the earth and is doomed to wander in limbo (Orellana, 1990). They are of such importance that while other aspects of the wake, like the unique decoration of the room, or the special clothes of the child could be omitted, the songs can not (Orellana, 1990). The words from the 'versos por angelitos' are believed to have an actual power to transform the child into an angel and the act of singing them gives the words even greater power to communicate with 'the other side', the supernatural (Orellana, 1990).

The wake begins with 'verses of greeting' addressed to the 'angelito'. Other music not unique to the 'velorio de angelito' and not necessarily of spiritual significance may later be played, with some regions of Latin America also including dancing at some stage of the proceedings (Dannemann, 2007; Schechter, 1983). Then at dawn just before transporting the child to the cemetery for burial, farewell verses are sung. In those verses the 'angelito' addresses the mourners as if present and takes leave of his family. In Chile, it is the verses of greeting and farewell that are considered instrumental in bringing about the desired transformation of the child to the state of an angel (Orellana, 1990).

While the rituals are less popular in modern times, they can still be observed in more rural areas of Chile (Dannemann, 2007). In addition, contemporary musicians have shown an interest in the genre. Twentieth-century compositions of 'cantos de ángeles' by people such as Violetta Parra have been composed. Modern-day musicians like Inti-Illimani, Jaime Barria and Soledad Guarda from the band Bordemar have also created re-versioned recordings of the original 'cantos de ángeles' suitable for use within a more contemporary setting, using modern instruments like electronic keyboards.

Cross-Case Comparisons and Modern Secular Funerals

The secularisation of funerals is a phenomenon that is occurring in many parts of the world (Emke, 2002). Western societies entered a period in the latter half of the twentieth century when traditional rituals were waning in popularity and there were few substitutes available to the bereaved (Emke, 2002; Jalland, 2006; Klass, Silverman & Nickman, 1996). This deterioration in the role of rituals often led to insufficient grieving and inadequate grief resolution (Romanoff & Terenzio, 1998).

However, despite increased secularisation, rituals are increasingly becoming a part of the grieving process once again. Emke (2002) describes this growing trend towards personalisation of funerals as a 're-ritualization of the secular funeral' (p. 274). Cook and Walter (2005) argue that people now often use rituals of their own devising or radically revise traditional ones. Even when still conducted within a church setting, funerals now tend to be highly personalised rather than following traditional church procedure (Cook & Walter, 2005; Emke, 2002, p. 269). This was evident in the widely broadcast funeral of Princess Diana at Westminster Abbey in 1997, which despite being conducted in the setting of the Anglican church and using traditional liturgy and music, also contained more personal tributes such as the singing of 'Candle in the Wind' by Elton John (Garces-Foley & Holcomb, 2005).

Kastenbaum (2004) argues that, despite the loss of many traditional rituals in contemporary society, we still have three things in common with bereaved people throughout time: (i) the desire to feel that our loved one is 'all right' even though dead; (ii) the need to continue a feeling of connection to the deceased; and (iii) a need to somehow keep something of that person alive in us so that we can continue to show our love and respect. Kastenbaum argues that the living can only move confidently ahead with their own lives if they feel they have succeeded in those three areas.

60 *Sandra Garrido and Waldo F. Garrido*

An examination of the three music-based funeral rituals discussed above and others seems to indicate that music can fulfil a number of valuable psychological functions in the resolution of grief including those mentioned by Kastenbaum. We will discuss each of these functions in turn with references to the above examples.

Funeral Music and Coping Strategies

Grief-coping strategies are often divided into task-focused (or problem-focused), and emotion focused behaviour (Anderson *et al.*, p. 812). Problem-focused coping involves active planning or engagement in behaviour to overcome distress (Schnider, Elhai & Gray, 2007). Emotion-focused behaviour involves attempts to regulate one's emotions and can be either adaptive, such as venting or cognitive reframing, or avoidant and maladaptive, such as denial or self-distraction (Schnider *et al.*, 2007).

In general, task-based coping appears to be the one most associated with positive grief outcomes, with emotion-based coping demonstrating a less consistently positive outcome (Nolen-Hoeksema, Parker & Larson, 1994). Avoidance can be useful early in the grieving process but can be less effective or even problematic if it continues in the long term (Schnider *et al.*, 2007). Some researchers suggest that a healthy balance of all three strategies is the most effective (Anderson *et al.*, 2005).

Corr *et al.* (2008) thus argue that funerals are a 'task-based' coping strategy because they allow the bereaved to take actions to begin to deal with the reality of the death and to ensure that the life of the deceased is remembered and celebrated. Music again plays a key role in this.

In the context of the jazz funeral and the contemporary funerals of many Afro-American communities, the providing of music and the participation in its performance allows the bereaved to feel that they have demonstrated the value of the deceased and expressed their affection for them effectively. Similarly, in the case of Georgian laments, the biographical nature of the laments allows the grievers to feel that they have marked the loss of the deceased in a meaningful way and expressed their affection for them. Both in Georgia and in communities using the jazz funeral, it is believed that the quality of the farewell provided, including the music, helps to ensure the place of the deceased in the afterlife. Similarly, in Chile the hiring of the 'cantors' provides a task-based strategy for dealing with grief in that the mourners believe that through the music they are assisting the child's transformation to a better state.

The selection of music for use in modern funerals can also be a meaningful task for the bereaved. By means of it, the bereaved (or the deceased themselves) communicate a message about the person, their importance to their loved ones, and their relationships with others. This music then acts as an enduring symbol of the person in the minds of those who have attended the funeral. Those who are left behind are comforted to think that the deceased will be remembered in a particular way.

Continuing Bonds with the Deceased

Over the past one hundred years, emphasis has commonly been put on arriving at 'closure' and severing one's attachment to the deceased (Klass & Goss, 1999). However, Silverman & Klass (1996) suggest that successful resolution of grief lies not in letting go, but in internalising and incorporating aspects of the lost person. While individuals have differing needs in relation to grief and some people may benefit from detaching from the deceased (Stroebe, Schut & Boerner, 2010), other bereaved people cope by clinging to memories of the deceased (Jalland, 2006).

Arguably, music can play an important role in fulfilling these functions within the context of a funeral, in much the same way that material objects can. The people of the northern Ecuadorian highland Quichua of Cotacachi, for example, share food with their deceased child, thus creating a sense of ongoing connection with them (Schechter, 1983). In Western societies it is quite typical to leave flowers or gifts at a grave site, a similar gesture of an ongoing relationship. Holloway (2007) argues that the use of physical objects to memorialise the deceased provides a focus for 'social transition' as well as a 'psychological and spiritual link' between the living and the dead (p. 161). Thus for some, physical memorials may serve as tools for moving forward with their lives. For others they may be a way of continuing their bonds with the deceased.

Music can similarly provide a sense of ongoing connection with the deceased and therefore a feeling that the deceased still exists in some way. One way that it does so is by acting as a trigger for memories of the deceased and for bringing back vivid images and feelings associated with the deceased (Caswell, 2011–2012; DeNora, 2003). O'Callaghan *et al.* (2013) reported that some participants in their study were unexpectedly comforted when hearing the funeral music on later occasions since it allowed them to feel the deceased's presence or to be reminded of their message. The music itself therefore creates a sense of an ongoing relationship with the deceased since it is able to invoke powerful emotions and memories connected with the deceased. Given its emotive and symbolic powers, music therefore has the potential to be an even more effective tool for creating continuing bonds with the deceased than material objects.

All three of the mourning traditions considered in this article involve the belief that the music is an integral part of providing an appropriate farewell for the bereaved and thus ensuring their favourable reception in the afterlife. In Chile it is also traditionally believed that the deceased child will continue to act as an intercessor with the spirit world on behalf of the family who enables their transition to spirit life in this way (Orellana, 1990). This is another way in which the music in those contexts assists the bereaved to feel a sense of ongoing connection with the deceased.

Celebrating the Life of the Deceased

Moules (1998) argues that although sorrow is a part of grief, grief also encompasses a celebration of the deceased. Both the jazz funeral and the Chilean 'cantos

62   *Sandra Garrido and Waldo F. Garrido*

de ángeles' involve music intended to celebrate the occasion rather than mourn. While not all mourners in modern Western contexts have similar beliefs that death is a transition to a better life, contemporary mourners at times prefer to focus on celebrating the good life that the deceased enjoyed than on the loss they have suffered (Castle & Philips, 2003). Thus modern funerals in Western countries often display picture boards or treasured items belonging to the deceased. Music played may be music that was of special significance to the deceased rather than music that might have been traditionally used at a funeral service (Wouters, 2002). This music might even seem out of place or somewhat irreverent at an occasion of mourning. However, in their choice of music, the bereaved are enabled to celebrate and memorialise the life of the deceased in a very individual way.

Facilitating the Expression of Grief and Sharing it with Others

Funerals in general provide a vehicle for both the expression and containment of strong emotions, providing an opportunity for the display of grief plus a structure for its delimitation (Romanoff & Terenzio, 1998), and it is arguable that the music used on the occasion enhances this effect. Since music's power to touch the emotions is one of its most important functions in human society generally (Juslin & Västfjäll, 2008), its capacity to provoke tears and therefore facilitate expression of grief is of great value in the context of mourning. Recent studies have shown that in therapy situations music can help validate and express the emotions associated with grief (Dalton & Krout, 2005; Hilliard, 2001). Bright (1995) thus argues that music offers a 'passport to the heart' (p. 323) and as such can offer many advantages over comforts dependent on words. Thus in the context of mourning rituals, music may have similar benefits.

One of the primary evolutionary functions which music is believed to have served is the promotion of social bonding (Dunbar & Dunbar, 1998). DeNora (2000) argues that in a group setting, music can act on the emotions of the listeners and draw them together in the shared experience of those emotions. A similar function operates in the context of the funeral. The music of laments in Georgia provide a 'ritual of shared grieving' (Kotthoff, 2001, p. 191) in which the loss of a loved one is communalised and vocalised for the benefit of all the mourners present. This public outpouring of grief is a catalyst for the healing process (Kotthoff, 2001). While the lamenters themselves keep control over their emotions, the listeners are commonly provoked to tears. The lamenting of the women thus frees the grief of the listeners (Kotthoff, 2006), enabling some catharsis.

In relation to the 'velorio del angelito', Schechter (1983) states that the atmosphere of a fiesta creates an illusion of normality which seeks to 'entrap particularly the mother and the godparents in a net of emphatic joy, thus saving them from the freedom to grieve' (p. 52). At the same time, he argues, at an event like this 'the emotions are already aroused [and] supercharge[ed]' (p. 55) and the music gives direction to and allows an outlet for these emotions.

The music also serves to join mourners together in remembering the deceased in a particular way (Cook & Walter, 2005). In the case of the jazz funeral, performance of the music and participation in the parades joins the community together in celebrating the life of the deceased and the new life that it is believed they will now attain. Secundy (1989) reports that the funeral rituals of Afro-Americans of the jazz funeral tradition are 'vitally important for helping blacks maintain mental health. They enhance self-acceptance, acceptance of others, and acceptance of nature . . . The black church and black music, in or out of church, allow catharsis, survival, and coping . . . ' (p. 100).

In Georgia, too, the collaborative nature of lamenting enables a sense of sharing the loss within the community (Kotthoff, 2001), thus strengthening social ties as well as making the bereaved feel less alone in their loss. In Chile, the ritual similarly improves solidarity in the local community as they come together to share the music and to share their grief (Schechter, 1994). Thus collective musical grieving in each of the cultural contexts discussed in this chapter facilitates mutual expression of emotions within the community, enhancing group cohesion and enabling the grievers to feel joined in mourning with those around them.

Redefining Personal Narratives

The funeral is a period of transition for the bereaved during which they must begin to turn their attention to learning to live with the changes that have occurred. A core part of healing after the death of a loved one is the task of making sense of the loss, finding meaning in the death of the loved one, and reconstructing the narrative of one's life in light of the bereavement (Neimeyer, 2001). Gillies and Neimeyer (2006) propose that there are three particular aspects to this finding of meaning in the aftermath of the loss: sense making, benefit finding and identity change. The bereaved must assimilate their changed relationship with the deceased into their current lives (Humphrey & Zimpfer, 2008). They are encouraged by counsellors to redefine their own identity with awareness that their past relationship with the deceased is an integral part of who they have become (Klass, Silverman & Nickman, 1996).

Music both forms part of the narrative of loss itself, and can help to shape the emerging personal narrative of the bereaved. In the case of the Georgian lament, the music is a spontaneous, individualised narration of the life of the deceased and his/her relationships with others. In the case of the jazz funeral and the 'cantos de ángeles', the use of traditional musical texts reiterates the beliefs of the hereafter and enunciates the changed situation of the bereaved. It thus helps to formulate the shifting personal narrative of those left behind.

Given the strong associations between music and identity (Connell & Gibson, 2003; Hargreaves, Miell & MacDonald, 2002; Ruud, 1997), and its capacity for triggering memories, the music played at the funeral can tell the story of the deceased and of those who mourn them, thus assisting the bereaved to begin to formulate their shifting self-view in light of their loss. In modern contexts where music choices may be highly personalised, music has the potential to serve this function with even greater force. The music of the funeral itself becomes entwined within the narrative of the deceased's life and that of the mourners.

64   *Sandra Garrido and Waldo F. Garrido*

A Catalyst for Confronting the Fact of the Loss

Schechter (1994) argues that the rituals associated with the 'velorio del angelito' allow time for the bereaved to adjust their minds to the altered condition of the deceased. The actions of treating the child as if still alive, being washed, dressed and spoken to in song allows the survivors to adjust gradually (Schechter, 1994). Dressing the child as an angel and then assisting the child's transition to an angelic state with music allows the family to enact their hope in the child's future. This would have the benefit both of helping the family to understand the reality of the death and to overcome denial and shock, and to soften the blow with their hopes for the child's continued happiness.

In all its cultural variations, the funeral serves as a symbolic enactment of the transition of the loved one from life to death (Romanoff & Terenzio, 1998). The act of singing about the death or the deceased can thus assist the bereaved to gradually adjust to the fact of the death. The ritual laments in Georgian culture also force the bereaved to confront the reality of what has occurred. In modern funerals too, music has the potential to bring thoughts of the deceased and the fact that they are gone to the forefront of the minds of all present at the funeral.

Reinforcing Religious Conviction and Creating an Atmosphere of Sacredness

Studies have shown that religion is often a strong support to those who are mourning (Balk, 1997). Anderson *et al.* (2005), for example, examined the interaction between psychological coping and religious coping and found that when taken together task-oriented grieving and positive religious coping resulted in a significant positive association with lower self-reported grief (p. 823). In situations where traditional religious music is used in the funeral, mourners are reminded of their conviction in an afterlife and the hope that such beliefs can give them is thus reinforced. The three traditional music genres discussed above all hold strong connections to the spiritual beliefs of the communities in which they are used.

However, music can create an atmosphere of sacredness even in secular settings. Many bereaved, no matter how secular in outlook, will likely continue to take comfort from the belief that the deceased now exists in a better place or that the deceased continues to exist in some way (Jalland, 2006). The selection of music that expresses their own personal beliefs about death can strengthen such hopes, providing further comfort to some.

Aside from its association with any beliefs the bereaved may hold, music can imbue any occasion with a sense of the special, something which can make the bereaved feel that the passing of their loved one is being given the weight that it deserves. It is inherently associated with experiences of the spiritual even in secular contexts (Palmer, 2006; Penman & Becker, 2009). Music can also be a powerful trigger for memories (Batcho, 2007), and can thus come to hold a strong symbolic significance of past relationships and events. Klass and Goss (1999) argue that the means by which bonds are continued with the deceased, such as

The Psychological Function of Music in Mourning Rituals   65

objects, memory or visions of the deceased, have a spiritual quality about them. Music could be said to be the same. Even though there is less belief in the modern world in the magical powers of music to transform, the necessity still exists for rituals, albeit more secularised ones, and a sense of the sacred to surround the death of a loved one. It is therefore an important vehicle for instilling occasions of mourning with the symbolic and the sacred. This can be so whether the music choices are traditional or modern.

Concluding Remarks

Music used in funerals has developed in recent years in a life-interpreting direction and this reflects important changes in the approach to questions of life and death. Music has been a significant part of rituals for centuries and thus has an important role to play in 'coping and self-healing with words and song' (Secundy, 1989, p. 104). Castle and Philips (2003) express the hope that the creation of new, personal rituals will enable many to 'make room in their lives for a relationship with grief, to learn and grow from that relationship' (p. 62).

The function of music within modern-day grief rituals is thus an important area warranting further investigation in future research. Such research would look at specific music choices for use in contemporary funerals and its significance both to the bereaved and to the deceased person who may have chosen it, exploring further the potential for music to play a healing role in the lives of the grievers. Questions of particular interest in future studies may be the value of music in giving the bereaved a sense of celebrating the life of the deceased and in establishing feelings of ongoing connection with them. Of further consideration would be how music choices are influenced by individual differences in coping styles. Such research could further illuminate current approaches to death and mourning in contemporary society as well as provide some further understanding of the power music has had within rituals across time and culture.

References

Anderson, M. J., Marwit, S. J., Vandenberg, B., & Chibnall, J. T. (2005). Psychological and Religious Coping Strategies of Mothers Bereaved by the Sudden Death of a Child. *Death Studies, 29*, 811–826.

Balk, D. E. (1997). Death, bereavement and college students: a descriptive analysis. *Mortality, 2*(3), 207–220.

Batcho, K. I. (2007). Nostalgia and the emotional tone and content of song lyrics. *The American Journal of Psychology, 120*(3), 361–381.

Becker, J. (2001). Anthropological perspectives on music and emotion. In P. Juslin & J. Sloboda (Eds.), *Music and Emotion* (pp. 135–160). Oxford: Oxford University Press.

Bright, R. (1995). Music therapy as a facilitator in grief counselling. In T. Wigram & B. Saperston (Eds.), *The Art & Science of Music Therapy: A Handbook*. London and New York: Routledge.

Castle, J., & Philips, W. L. (2003). Grief rituals: Aspects that facilitate adjustment to bereavement. *Journal of Loss and Trauma, 8*(1), 41–71.

66 Sandra Garrido and Waldo F. Garrido

Caswell, G. (2011–2012). Beyond words: Some uses of music in the funeral setting. *OMEGA: Journal of Death and Dying, 64*(4), 319–334.

Collins, W. L., & Doolittle, A. (2006). Personal reflections on funeral rituals and spirituality in a Kentucky African American family. *Death Studies, 30*, 957–969.

Connell, J., & Gibson, C. (2003). *Sound Tracks: Popular Music, Identity and Place*. London and New York: Routledge.

Cook, G., & Walter, T. (2005). Rewritten rites: language and social relations in traditional and contemporary funerals. *Discourse and Society, 16*(3), 365–391.

Corr, C. A., Nabe, C., Nabe, C. M., & Corr, D. M. (2008). *Death and Dying, Life and Living*. Belmont, CA: Cengage Learning.

Dalton, T. A., & Krout, R. E. (2005). Development of the grief process scale through music therapy songwriting with bereaved adolescents. *The Arts in Psychotherapy, 32*, 131–143.

Dannemann, M. (2007). *Cultura Folclorica de Chile* (Vol. 1). Santiago, Chile: Editorial Universitaria.

DeNora, T. (2000). *Music in Everyday Life*. Cambridge: Cambridge University Press.

DeNora, T. (2003). *After Adorno: Rethinking Music Sociology*. Cambridge: Cambridge University Press.

Doss, E. (2006). Spontaneous memorials and contemporary modes of mourning in America. *Material Religion, 2*(3), 294–319.

Dunbar, R., & Dunbar, R. I. M. (1998). *Grooming, gossip, and the evolution of language*: Harvard University Press.

Emke, I. (2002). Why the sad face? Secularization and the changing function of funerals in Newfoundland. *Mortality, 7*(3), 269–284.

Emsheimer, E. (1967). Georgian folk polyphony. *Journal of the International Folk Music Council, 19*, 54–57.

Feld, S. (2012). *Sound and Sentiment: Birds, Weeping, Poetics, and Song in Kaluli Expression* (3rd ed.). Durham, NC: Duke University Press.

Garces-Foley, K., & Holcomb, J. S. (2005). Personalizing Tradition. In K. Garces-Foley (Ed.), *Death and Religion in a Changing World* (pp. 207–277). Armonk, NY: M.E. Smharpe.

Garrido, S., & Garrido, W. (2011). *The folklore of death: 'Cantos de angeles' and cultural syncretism on the island of Chiloe*. Paper presented at the 7th International Small Islands Cultures Conference, Airlie Beach, Australia.

Gillies, J., & Neimeyer, R. (2006). Loss, grief, and the search for significance: Toward a model of meaning reconstruction in bereavement. *Journal of Constructivist Psychology, 19*(1), 31–65.

Goss, R., & Klass, D. (1997). Tibetan Buddhism and the resolution of grief: The Bardo-Thodol for the dying and the grieving. *Death Studies, 21*(4), 377–395.

Hargreaves, D. J., Miell, D., & MacDonald, R. A. R. (2002). What are musical identities and why are they important? In R. A. R. MacDonald (Ed.), *Musical Identities* (pp. 1–20). Oxford: Oxford University Press.

Hilliard, R. E. (2001). The effects of music-therapy based bereavement groups on mood and behavior of grieving children: a pilot study. *Journal of Music Therapy, 38*(4), 291–306.

Holloway, M. (2007). *Negotiating death in contemporary health and social care*. Bristol: Policy Press.

Humphrey, G. M., & Zimpfer, D. G. (2008). *Counselling for Grief and Bereavement* (2nd ed.). London: SAGE Publications Ltd.

Jalland, P. (2006). *Changing ways of death in twentieth-century Australia: war, medicine and the funeral business*. Sydney: UNSW Press.

The Psychological Function of Music in Mourning Rituals   67

Juslin, P. N., & Västfjäll, D. (2008). Emotional response to music: the need to consider underlying mechanisms. *Behavioral and Brain Sciences, 31*, 559–621.

Kastenbaum, R. (2004). Why funerals? *Generations, 28*(2), 5–10.

Klass, D., & Goss, R. (1999). Spiritual bonds to the dead in cross-cultural and historical perspective: Comparative religion and modern grief. *Death Studies, 23*(6), 547–567.

Klass, D., Silverman, P. R., & Nickman, S. L. (1996). *Continuing bonds: new understandings of grief.* Taylor & Francis.

Kotthoff, H. (2001). Verbal Art Across Cultures: The Aesthetics and Proto-aesthetics of Communication. In H. Knobloch & H. Kotthoff (Eds.), *Aesthetic dimensions of Georgian grief rituals: On the artful display of emotions in lamentation* (pp. 167–194). Tubingen: Gunter Narr Verlag.

Kotthoff, H. (2006). Communicating affect in intercultural lamentations in Caucasian Georgia. In K. Buhrig & J. D. T. Thije (Eds.), *Beyond Misunderstanding: Linguistic Analyses of Intercultural Communication.* Amsterdam: JoÛ Benjamins Publishing.

McIlwain, C. D. (2003). *Death in black and white: death, ritual and family ecology:* Hampton Press.

Moules, N. J. (1998). Legitimizing grief: Challenging beliefs that constrain. *Journal of Family Nursing, 4*(2), 142–166.

Nakashidze, K. (2002). *On polyphony in Georgian funeral songs.* Paper presented at the First International Symposium on Traditional Polyphony, Tbilisi, Georgia.

Neimeyer, R. (2001). Reauthoring life narratives: Grief therapy as meaning reconstruction. *The Israel Journal of Psychiatry and Related Sciences, 28*(3–4), 171–183.

Nolen-Hoeksema, S., Parker, L. E., & Larson, J. (1994). Ruminative coping with depressed mood following loss. *Journal of Personality and Social Psychology, 67*(1), 92–104.

O'Callaghan, C., McDermott, F., Hudson, P., & Zalcberg, J. R. (2013). Sound continuing bonds with the deceased: The relevance of music, including preloss music therapy, for eight bereaved caregivers. *Death Studies, 37*(2), 101–125.

Orellana, M. (1990). *Versos por Angelito:* Poetry and its function at the wake of a peasant child in Chile. *Journal of Folklore Research, 27*(3), 191–203.

Palmer, A. J. (2006). Music education and spirituality: Philosophical exploration II. *Philosophy of Music Education Review, 14*(6), 143–158.

Penman, J., & Becker, J. (2009). Religious ecstatics, 'deep listeners', and musical emotion. *Empirical Musicology Review, 4*(2), 49–70.

Reeves, N. C., & Boersma, F. J. (1989–1990). The therapeutic use of ritual in maladaptive grieving. *Journal of Death and Dying, 20*(4), 281–291.

Romanoff, B. D., & Terenzio, M. (1998). Rituals and the grieving process. *Death Studies, 22*(8), 697–711.

Ruud, E. (1997). Music and Identity. *Nordic Journal of Music Therapy, 6*(1), 3–13.

Sakakeeny, M. (2011). Jazz funerals and second line parades. In D. JoÛson (Ed.), *KnowLA Encyclopedia of Louisiana*: Louisiana Endowment for the Humanities.

Schechter, J. M. (1983). Corona y Baile: Music in the Child's Wake of Ecuador and Hispanic South America. Past and Present. *Latin American Music Review/Revista de Musica Latinoamericana, 4*(1), 1–80.

Schechter, J. M. (1994). Divergent Perspectives on the Velorio Del Angelito. *Journal of Ritual Studies, 8*(2), 43–84.

Schechter, J. M. (2009). Latin America/Chile, Bolivia, Ecuador, Peru. In J. T. Titon (Ed.), *Worlds of Music: An Introduction to the Music of the World's Peoples* (5th ed.). Belmont, CA: Schirmer Cengage Learning.

68 *Sandra Garrido and Waldo F. Garrido*

ScÛider, K. R., Elhai, J. D., & Gray, M. J. (2007). Coping style use predicts posttraumatic stress and complicated grief symptom severity among college students reporting a traumatic loss. *Journal of Counseling Psychology, 54*(3), 344–350.

Secundy, M. G. (1989). Coping with words and song: The New Orleans jazz funeral. *Literature and Medicine, 8*, 100–105.

Silverman, P. R., & Klass, D. (1996). Introduction: What's the problem? In D. Klass, P. R. Silverman & S. L. Nickman (Eds.), *Continuing Bonds: New Understandings of Grief.* Philadelphia: Taylor & Francis.

Stroebe, M., Schut, H., & Boerner, K. (2010). Continuing bonds in adaptation to bereavement: Toward theoretical integration. *Clinical Psychology Review, 30*(2), 259–268.

Woodthorpe, K. (2011). Using bereavement theory to understand memorialising behaviour. *Bereavement Care, 30*(2), 29–32.

Wouters, C. (2002). The quest for new rituals in dying and mourning: Changes in the we-I balance. *Body and Society, 8*(1), 1–27.

7 'Under the Bruised Sky'

Music and Mourning in Post-revolutionary Iran[1]

Sarah Walker

If you have not seen a crazy person,
look! they call us crazy.

We used to be normal,
but the love of Hossein made us crazy.

My logic has been taken by God,
the love of Hossein has taken over instead

Everyone has a friend in his heart,
in our heart, it's Hossein that is the friend

Everyone has a tranquil song,
the song in my heart is Yaa Hossein.

Traditional *nohe*, translated by Mohammad Panahi

Melodic mourning, or elegiac singing (*nohe khani* in Persian), is a central feature of Shi'a Islam, the dominant faith of Iran. *Nohe khani* is performed primarily in honour of Shi'a Imams, by a professional mourner known as a *Maddah*, and traditionally in communal contexts, enabling sociability and the sharing of spiritual and personal grief, as participants weep for recent losses as well as those of the distant past. In recent decades, Iran's turbulent history has seen shifts in the contexts and significance of *nohe khani*. Iran's 1979 revolution was closely followed by the Iran–Iraq war (1980–1988), which devastated both countries and left few, if any, families untouched by the high rate of casualties, mostly young men and boys who had volunteered to fight. The war saw the *Maddah*'s activities expand from comfortable community gatherings to the violent, masculine, fearful space of the front. At the same time, the melodies and rhythms of *nohe khani* were adapted to their new context. In the twenty-first century, the *Maddah*'s performance contexts have expanded again, as many young *nohe khani* fans embrace

---

1 'Under the bruised sky' is a line from a traditional *nohe* frequently recited at mourning ceremonies in Iran. I am very grateful to the many colleagues and friends who assisted with this research and to the referees for their helpful comments.

70   Sarah Walker

the simultaneously private and public sphere of the internet. While professional mourners continue to facilitate communal grieving, the ensuing forms of sociability and sharing of emotions are quite different. This chapter examines some of the changes around elegiac singing in Iran since 1979, as well as aspects of the emotional, spiritual and social lives of its participants.

Since the advent of online media such as *YouTube*, the music video has become one of the most widely circulated forms of audiovisual representation. In the case of the Islamic Republic of Iran, this has enabled not only the circulation of music that has not been granted official authorization by Iran's government, but also the decontextualized visual representation of Islamic 'musical' forms such as *nohe khani*. There is an extensive range of videos of *nohe khani* on the internet. Until the twenty-first century, *nohe khani* was performed in communal contexts, at moments considered particularly appropriate, including commemoration of the Imams, funerals and the war front. There was no notion of a *nohe khani* fan-base until this century, when it became possible to decontextualize performances. Visual representations have become an increasingly significant component of this decontextualization and a factor in *nohe khani* fans' preferences. Only a minority of Iran's postrevolutionary generation would claim to be *nohe khani* fans, but that minority is diverse and it plays an important role in Iran's cultural memory.

After considering the broader context of *Maddahi* in urban, postwar Iran, I will examine the ways the management, fans and detractors of one young Tehrani *Maddah*, known as Abdol Reza Helali, have used and/or responded to representations of the professional religious singer. Focusing on photographs adapted for websites, posters and DVD covers, I argue that many young fans respond to images that evoke a fashionable romanticism and a sense of spiritual superiority or 'Islamic cool'. The *Maddah*'s management promotes such images, online and elsewhere. Meanwhile, some detractors of this 'pop *Maddah*' point to the perceived paradoxes of representations they see as flippant and essentially commercial. This chapter is based on fieldwork conducted in Iran from 2007 to 2012. As well as attending and observing mourning ceremonies, I conducted interviews and conversations with *Maddah*s and others who take part in such commemorations. Two male colleagues in Tehran also generously conducted interviews on my behalf with some men working in various roles relating to *Maddahi*, in some cases because the men preferred not to speak directly with me. As many of our informants prefer not to be quoted directly, I present much of the information gained through this fieldwork in a generalized form.

The *Hosseinieh*: Watching Martyrs, Hidden *Maddah*

An enduring venue for *Maddahi* is the *Hosseinieh*, a centre dedicated to the rituals of commemoration of Imam Hossein. The Prophet Mohammad's grandson, Imam Hossein was killed as a young man at Karbala, in modern Iraq, in the seventh century. Imam Hossein is the central figure in the long Shi'a history of martyrdom. Among other things, he represents courageous perseverance in the face of brutal injustice and he is venerated as a defender of morality in an immoral world. Imam

'Under the Bruised Sky' 71

Hossein is also the central figure in *nohe* lyrics. In August 2007, I attended a meeting in a Hosseinieh in eastern Tehran, at which Abdol Reza Helali performed as Maddah. It was the birthday of Imam Mahdi, the *Imam-e Zaman* or last Imam, who is expected by believers to return to earth in the 'last days', bringing justice and an end to oppression. Although the event was primarily a celebration of the last Imam, the Maddah's repertoire focused just as much, if not more, on Imam Hossein and Imam Ali, the first Imam and father of Hossein.

The Hosseinieh had three floors; the walls of each were covered with photographs of relatively recent martyrs – young men and boys who died in the Iran–Iraq war. On the top floor, which was reserved for women, there was a dispute before the ceremony began. The woman who sat at the door argued that all women in attendance should wear chadors, while some of the younger women felt that minimal hijab was sufficient, as no men were present. At this, the older woman gestured towards the walls and said that the martyrs were watching. This moment in the Hosseinieh illustrates aspects of the often paradoxical roles that visual representations can play. The argument that images of the dead may represent a form of active gaze, or seeing presence, reflects, among other things, the authority or power often attached to the visual. Of course, the ways authority is attached vary, among individuals and between different generations. Images of war martyrs are perhaps the most visible representations in Iran's public domain. For some, who view the martyrs' sacrifice as the foundation stone of the Islamic Republic, martyrs' images are also representations *of* Iran. Others see the war martyrs' lives and deaths as a reflection of the lives and deaths of the Imams, through whom the Shi'a faith was formed and whose images and names are also attributed authority and power. Of course, for families and others who knew martyrs personally, their images also dominate the private domain and play quite different roles. The 'power' of these images naturally depends in part on the viewer's relationship with and/or memories of the war and those who fought it. For many members of the postwar generation, murals and other large images of martyrs are as much a part of their everyday environment as advertising billboards – or, as one young Tehrani puts it, 'like trees' (personal communication, 2008) – and, as such, disregarded.

While it was considered proper that the women on the Hosseinieh's top floor should see the martyrs' images (whether or not the martyrs could 'see' us), it was not considered appropriate for us to see the living Helali. Helali performed, in front of a crowd of mostly young men, on the Hosseinieh's underground floor. A floor above, other men watched the performance on a screen. On the top floor, a large, mixed group of women, including the elderly, teenagers and women with small children, listened to the performance through speakers. A small circle of young women, dressed in fashionable hijab, sat on the floor in the centre of the room, clapping, singing loudly and weeping at appropriate moments in Helali's performance. One of these women appeared to verge on collapse at a particularly climactic moment. While we were not able to watch Helali in the flesh, we women have access to many representations of him performing as he performed that night. We can buy VCDs and DVDs; we can download the many videos on *YouTube*. Of course, when we watch recordings of a Maddah outside the context

72   Sarah Walker

of the Hosseinieh or other religious events, our roles as community members, participants and/or recipients of spiritual encouragement are transformed, as the Maddah's role is arguably decontextualized. When we engage with such recordings on the internet, we enter different communities, with different dynamics from those of a Hosseinieh. The comments on Helali's *YouTube* sites reflect the very broad range of responses viewers have to his recorded performances. These responses – from around the world – include gratitude, spiritual gratification, perplexed fascination and ridicule.

In Iran, as well as many fans, Helali has critics, including some who see his work as lacking musical skill and taste. He himself confirms his ignorance of the musical system on which *nohe khani* is traditionally based (Helali's then manager, personal communication, Tehran, 2007). Some of Helali's fellow Maddahs also criticize his style on spiritual grounds. One of these explains that a good Maddah, in effect, leads a collective process of 'making love' to the Imams he or she praises (Majid, personal communication, Tehran, 2007). To do this effectively, he or she should create and gradually intensify an atmosphere of love and grief. The performance style and the *nohe* pieces chosen should combine to build this atmosphere to an emotional peak (*shur*), which is simultaneously grief-stricken (at the death of the Imam) and euphoric (because of the perceived closeness to God – and the Imam – that this expression of grief achieves). An effective Maddah maintains this state as long as possible, before gently bringing the collective emotional performance back 'to earth'. In the case of Helali, some fellow Maddahs criticize his timing, suggesting that it reflects that of the young generation's popular culture. That is, rather than facilitating a slow, 'spiritual' climax, which would reflect the Maddah's humility, Helali intensifies the atmosphere early in his performance. This is seen as having the more self-serving effect of exciting the audience and focusing attention on Helali as performer rather than on the Imam and his death. Some fellow Maddahs and other mourners criticize Helali for borrowing melodies and rhythmic structures from secular pop music. He has often done this without subtlety, simply singing *nohes* to the melodies of popular songs, including several from the Los Angeles Persian pop genre.

Such strategies have had considerable success in popularizing *nohe khani* among some sections of the postrevolutionary generation. However, the essentially mournful nature of commemorating the dead, including martyrs, and the Imams, does not appeal to all. In August 2009, a self-identified 'middle-class, young Iranian' wrote:

> A few weeks ago was the birthday of one of Shiism's most important figures, the imam in occultation, the Messiah who will one day rid this world of corruption and injustice . . . You turned on the TV and a mournful voice scratched your ear. You wondered if this occasion was meant to bring happiness to citizens. It seems that we are invited to fear the coming of the Messiah rather than appreciate his bringing balance to the world. (Saeedi, 2009)

While this young author's central argument is not directed primarily at Maddahi, it is an example of the diversity of approaches to this form and its contexts among the postrevolutionary generation. For some young Iranians, the Maddah represents only misery and fear – or boredom and poor taste; for others, especially those attracted to audiovisual representations of pop Maddahs such as Helali, he or she represents a spiritual cool and a form of passion that encompasses happiness.

The Visible Man

In Ralph Ellison's novel *Invisible Man*, the narrator reflects on the sounds of a song performed by Louis Armstrong, 'What did I do to be so black and blue?' (Razaf, Waller and Brooks, 1929). Referring to Armstrong and his trumpet, he writes: 'Louis bends that military instrument into a beam of lyrical sound' (Ellison, 1952, p. 6). The 'bending' of an instrument's significance from militarism into lyricism serves as a useful metaphor for some cultural practices in postwar Iran. For example, practices around *nohe khani* that were explicitly employed to motivate young men to fight in the 1980s may now be employed to transport young women and men into what some see as lyrical, semi-mystical experiences. While the aural is the crucial element of *nohe khani*, the visual is also significant in the transition from militaristic associations to forms of lyricism – even when the associated images are remembered or imagined by the listener, rather than 'seen'. Walter Benjamin suggests that one 'who has once begun to open the fan of memory never comes to the end of its segments. No image satisfies him, for he has seen that it can be unfolded, and only in its folds does the truth reside' (Benjamin, 1999, p. 597). This notion of the endless fan of memory is useful when considering Iran, its history of conflicts and the ways Iranians remember or evoke that history. When the Iran–Iraq war is remembered, its images unfold to reveal memories – or postmemory – of previous conflicts and mythologized martyrs. Even when the war is apparently forgotten, as has been the case for some Iranian youth, it re-emerges in the folds of other memories.

In contrast with Benjamin's view of history, some in Iran would argue that memory *does* have an 'end', which is simultaneously Shi'a history's 'beginning': the martyrdom of the brave young warrior Hossein at Karbala. According to one young Tehrani Maddah, Karbala is 'beyond time and space': it is the focal point of all history, to which its predecessors looked forward and subsequent generations look back (Majid, personal communication, 2007). The narrative of Hossein's death lurks around much collective memory in Iran and is especially present in *nohe khani*. *Nohe khani* increased in prominence during the Iran–Iraq war, primarily because it was performed at the front to encourage soldiers to persevere in the deadly fighting, but also because it was heard at the frequent funerals of those mostly young men who persevered and were killed. As a result, *nohe khani* diversified. Different Maddahs developed their own styles, as they sought to perform as effectively as possible and thereby contribute to the war effort. The Maddah's roles include spiritual encouragement, facilitation of mourning and the transmission of what they see as history, that is, the lives and deaths of the imams. All these tasks are performed by means of the Maddah's repertoire and modes of performance.

74 *Sarah Walker*

After the war, the Maddah's role gradually became less prominent in Iran. However, recent years have seen the return of the Maddah to significant roles in public life. These roles are somewhat different from those of the wartime Maddah, but they again involve the spiritual encouragement of young people. The majority of young people in Tehran do not regularly attend Hosseinieh meetings and are not fans of *nohe khani*. However, a significant minority – known as *heya'ati* or 'group members' – is as devoted to this form as their peers are to metal, rap or dance music. This minority's heroes are the Maddahs who sing at their meetings and who are represented as spiritual warriors. Images of these 'warriors' inspire their young fans in ways that images of the martyrs of their parents' generation may not.

The possibilities of decontextualization that have emerged with visual and online communications concern some observers of the Maddah's 'new' roles. Critics argue that the spiritual 'purpose' of *nohe khani* is distorted or lost when the Maddah takes on the role of entertainer (personal communication, Tehran, 2007). Especially since the Iran–Iraq war, the Maddah has been popularly represented in Iran as close to God, while authorities have represented entertainment as separate from and irrelevant to spiritual practice. However, it can be argued that this supposed separation of entertainment and spirituality has never, in reality, existed in Iran. William O. Beeman points out that:

> in Qajar Iran, the Maddah was considered to be an entertainer, and was licensed . . .
>
> The Maddah is an essential part of public life because the recitation of the events of the death of Imam Hussein is an essential part of Shi'a daily life . . . People endow weekly religious sessions in which the Maddah recites the Karbala story, and people weep. It verges on being a popular entertainment. (Beeman, 2007)

The Maddah's role as entertainer was transformed by the war, which raised him towards the level of 'saint' through his association with the martyrs. During and immediately after the war, there were many reasons for Iranians – both the state and sections of the population – to view entertainment as unseemly and inappropriate. However, for many members of the postwar generation, with its various forms of postmemory, entertainment and spirituality belong together. It could be argued that Helali's young fans are returning the Maddah to his traditional role of entertainer – or that his role never really changed. Rather, the *tone* of the Maddah's form of entertainment changed, in response to the context of revolution and a long, traumatic war.

The choice of some young fans to take their religious practices seriously is one of the ways they live with their postmemory of the war. Rejecting the apparent scepticism and perceived 'superficiality' of some other Iranian youth, they mourn with a fervour that is, at first glance, reminiscent of revolutionary fervour. However, unlike the revolutionary generation, Helali's young fans have not had

'Under the Bruised Sky' 75

to take part in actual warfare. Rather than mourning the fallen men and boys of their parents' generation, they 'remember' the mythologized martyrs of the distant past. Arguably, this may entail less of the idealism of an activist's response to injustice and more of a fashionable romanticism that is also a response to effective marketing. Along with the adoption of pop melodies and rhythms, Helali's management has promoted his work on the internet and elsewhere with images designed to attract young people. For example, unlike other Maddahs, he has often been photographed smiling.

The VCD cover shown in Figure 7.1 appeared in 2005 and illustrates the 'new' ways Maddahs may be represented to their youthful market. Here, Helali has what some see as sex appeal. The lighting emphasizes the post-performance perspiration on his forehead and hair. Helali's smile is boyish and verging on cheeky. The dark background suggests the intimate, enclosed environment of the Hosseinieh and, at the same time, leaves no space for peripheral references. Here, Helali is the star, simultaneously intimate and remote, casual and authoritative. For fans, this balance of intimacy and authority is cool – and Islamic. For Helali's management, it sells. However, some of Helali's detractors claim that a Maddah has no business smiling, promoting himself without a clear display of humility or potentially distracting mourners from the object of their religious practices. Other critics lament the perceived loss of the communal nature of mourning and object to the emphasis on individual gratification among young fans of the Maddah.

On the DVD cover shown in Figure 7.2, which appeared in 2006, Helali is represented as a 'serious' Maddah. His unsmiling – but not quite mournful – gaze,

Figure 7.1 The cover of Helali's *Moharram 1384* VCD (2005)

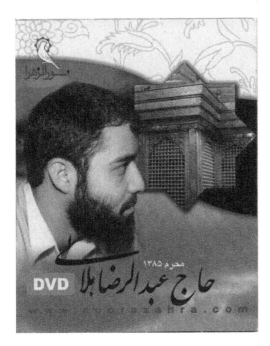

Figure 7.2 The cover of Helali's *Moharram 1385* DVD (2006)

away from the camera, suggests that his mind is on the spiritual and the invisible. Helali's neatly groomed hair and full beard are those of a Maddah not wishing to distract his audience from its spiritual objectives. The background colours are the red of the Imams' and martyrs' blood, the blue of the mosque and divinity and the black of mourning. While many fans would respond to this cover as a combination of appropriate spiritual references, some critics see an uninspired cut-and-paste of clichés (personal communication, Tehran). Some see a disproportionately large image of Helali, reflecting a perceived lack of proper humility, as well as an absence of representation of the traditionally communal nature of *nohe khani*.

In the website image shown in Figure 7.3, Helali appears as a young man with a hint of defiance in his facial expression and posture. The image lacks obvious spiritual references. Rather, it has an everyday, outdoor setting, with street cool. Helali could be sitting on the steps outside someone's home; his appearance and posture are casual. His direct gaze towards the camera suggests an engagement with his audience, rather than a spiritual focus. However, of course, the two are not mutually exclusive. The facial expression here is almost that of the 'Mona Lisa', simultaneously smiling and serious. Helali's version of Tehrani 'Islamic cool' is arguably evident in the hat that could serve as both an Islamic head cover and a fashionable beanie, the hair that curls over the hat and the collarless shirt of a young Islamic Iranian who, in contrast with some other sections of popular youth cultures in Tehran, demonstrates his indifference to so-called Western fashions.

Figure 7.3 Image of Helali on his 2007–2008 website, which also promoted 'Haj Abdorreza Helali' (sic) ringtones, www.behesht.info, accessed 22 August 2009

Figure 7.4 Profile picture for a *Facebook* group dedicated to Helali, 2009, www.facebook.com/group.php?gid=2529231710, accessed 22 August 2009

78 Sarah Walker

The image shown in Figure 7.4, chosen by fans for a *Facebook* group dedicated to Helali, represents the form of Islamic cool to which many such fans aspire. The colourful, kitsch aspects of some earlier images have gone. Helali's laughing, tilted face, his swaying posture and open hands, with the right palm facing upwards, suggest something of the 'craziness' of devotion to Hossein to which he refers in his *nohes*. A group administrator posted a *YouTube* video of Helali reciting *Age divoone nadidei* ('If you've never seen a crazy person'), along with the translation quoted in this article's epigraph, on the web page. However, while it is possible that the director of Helali's photograph shoot has drawn on popular imagery related to notions of a fashionable form of Sufism, the Maddah's 'craziness' differs from that of a mystic. In the above image, Helali's 'humility' and connection to Iranian tradition are represented by his cross-legged position

Figure 7.5 Reza Helali's *Facebook* profile picture, 2009, www.facebook.com/profile.php?id=100000075712376, accessed 22 August 2009

on the floor. However, this image also suggests control and authority, with the black, broad-shouldered coat contributing to the general effect of relatively neat elegance. There is no hint of Helali's usually visible perspiration or the busy environment of the communal Hosseinieh. The primary community addressed here is perhaps that of the internet, especially that section of Helali's fanbase that sees itself as sophisticated in its spirituality, its use of technology and its aesthetic preferences.

In 2009, fans of Helali selected the above image (Figure 7.5) for a *Facebook* profile set up in his name. Presumably, the photograph was taken when he undertook the Hajj pilgrimage, as he is wearing the required *ihram*. The *ihram* represents the equality of Muslims before God, as well as the pilgrim's devotion, purity and state of consecration. In Iran, the symbolism of the *ihram* has particular significance. As it also resembles a funeral shroud, it serves as a reminder of the Imams' and other martyrs' deaths. In 1963, in response to the arrest of Ayatollah Khomeini, people in Iran wrapped themselves in white to demonstrate their allegiance to the revolutionary leader and their readiness for martyrdom. Khomeini had been arrested after delivering a Moharram sermon, in which he likened the Iranian people's suffering to that of Imam Hossein.

The choice of the above image for Helali's personal identification suggests, perhaps, a desire to represent 'Haj Reza' the man, rather than just the Maddah. Where their comments are publicly visible, Helali's *Facebook* friends address him as 'Haj Reza'. While the image points to his personal devotion and humility, the 'holiness effect' is complicated – if not diminished – by the superimposition of his personal website address across his chest, from one shoulder to the other. Even here, while picturing the holiest pilgrimage, we are reminded of the commercial, technological world in which Helali and his generation live.

Helali himself, like most of his fans, was born during the Iran–Iraq war (in 1981). I turn now to aspects of this baby-boom generation's role in the ongoing construction of Iran's cultural memory. In visual and other forms, members of this generation articulate fluid understandings of martyrdom and applications of the narrative of Imam Hossein. Many urban Iranians of Helali's generation construct and respond to diverse notions of Islamic cool, along with the shifting cultural affiliations on which these notions depend.

The Children of War: Postmemory and Shifting Affiliations

> When I grew up, little by little I liked the word martyr. Not for its ideology though. There was something in it that I lacked: alliance building, paying a price for a better society. (Deghati, 2009)

Due to the postrevolutionary government's policies in the 1980s, there was a baby boom in Iran during the Iran-Iraq war. Iranian baby boomers are the children of war martyrs, veterans and their contemporaries. Helali and other members of this generation may be said to have a relationship of postmemory to the war into which they were born. Marianne Hirsch defines postmemory as:

80   *Sarah Walker*

> the response of the second generation to the trauma of the first . . . Postmemory
> most specifically describes the relationship of children of survivors of cul-
> tural or collective trauma to the experiences of their parents, experiences that
> they 'remember' only as the narratives and images with which they grew up,
> but that are so powerful, so monumental, as to constitute memories in their
> own right. (Hirsch, 2001, pp. 8–9)

The postrevolutionary generation grew up in an environment saturated with images of war martyrs and veterans. A high proportion of streets and public insti-tutions, from hospitals to schools, are named after martyrs. As Deghati reflects above, some who were too young for conscious involvement in the revolution or war felt that they 'lacked' the martyr's capacity for 'alliance building, pay-ing a price for a better society' – or they sensed that their elders regarded them as 'lacking'. It had seemed to some that nothing in the postrevolutionary gen-eration's relatively stable lives could compare with the memories of dramatic transformation, unprecedented mass solidarity, sweet triumph and bitter tragedy of the revolution and subsequent devastating war with Iraq. The heroes of this drama – as in the narratives recited in the Hosseinieh – were always the martyrs.

In this context, the somewhat playful nature of Helali's promotional methods invite new questions, while continuing to reflect the shifting mix of trends in his generation's cultural world. Helali has been described as 'the most popular Maddah' among Iran's *heya'ati* youth and as 'Iran's best Maddah' on *Facebook*. The night I heard him recite at the eastern Tehran Hosseinieh, I witnessed the nature of his popularity after the ceremony. As we all left the Hosseinieh, Helali was surrounded by a loud, excited crowd of young men, who pressed so closely around him that they seemed to be carrying him aloft. After Helali had left and some of us waited for taxis, one young man referred to Helali as his 'liver', an expression of extreme attachment and affection. Some youth apparently see Helali as a kind of spiritual guide, like other Maddahs. However, Helali often performs this role in the manner of a pop star. In this subcultural environment, closeness to Helali – and knowledge of the *nohes* he recites – gives young *heya'ati* social significance; it makes them – and their religious practices – cool.

In their attraction to the visual and other representations of what could be seen as a musical or subcultural fashion, Helali's 'religious' fans are arguably not so different from 'secular' members of their generation who are attracted to various forms of popular music in Tehran, such as alternative rock, so-called Sufi trance, rap, metal or dance pop. Some members of each of these groups take pride in their 'insider' – or 'outsider' – status; some see their particular musical forms of choice as spiritually or intellectually superior to others or as more exciting and cool. For example, various musical forms described as 'Sufi' are popular, especially among young people who are generally more affluent than most of Helali's fans. Some 'Sufi trance' fans claim to seek a 'gentler' spirituality than that of their govern-ment and of the men and boys who chose to go to war (personal communication, Tehran, 2008). They thus distance themselves from the perceived military mind-set of the revolution and war. Many such music fans 'remember' the war as futile

'*Under the Bruised Sky*' 81

and choose to 'forget' it or to reject its intrusion into the pleasure they take in music. By contrast, when Helali's fans glorify the ancient martyrs, surrounded by images of more recent martyrs, they may reconcile with their postmemory of both 'wars' by finding redemption in them. This does not mean that they necessarily desire war again; rather, for some, the only way to bear the terrible post/memory of war is to see it as a meaningful part of history. For these fans, *nohe khani* – like war – is almost unbearable in its evocation of grief, but may also be redemptive, as it brings mourners closer to God and the Imams. The 'pop' form of *nohe khani* favoured by *heya'ati* youth may be seen as part of a postwar approach that reconciles religiosity and individual gratification.

The ways cultural affiliations have shifted among Helali's generation in the twenty-first century are critical to representations of the past in Iran. Walter Benjamin imagines the 'angel of history' as one who faces the past:

> Where *we* see the appearance of a chain of events, *he* sees one single catastrophe, which unceasingly piles rubble on top of rubble and hurls it before his feet. He would like to stay, awaken the dead, and make whole what has been smashed. But a storm is blowing from Paradise, it has caught itself up in his wings and is so strong that the Angel can no longer close them. The storm drives him irresistibly into the future, to which his back is turned, while the rubble-heap before him grows sky-high. (Benjamin, 1992, 249)

In Iran, some who face the past would like to 'make whole' the revolutionary ideals – and much else – that were smashed by the war. But notions of Paradise, from those of 'believers' to those of 'pleasure-seekers' (and, of course, those who identify with both these characteristics), propel them into the future. As subsequent generations continue to reinvent their images of Paradise, they enable new forms of at least partial reconciliation. This reconciliation recognizes that 'what has been smashed' cannot be made whole and the dead cannot be awakened. However, the dead can still be 'mobilized' to provide their mourners with new forms of significance in an otherwise seemingly sceptical postwar Iran.

To conclude, I return to Louis Armstrong and a former *basiji* (paramilitary volunteer), a friend of mine who is not a *heya'ati*.[2] The last time I heard Armstrong's music was in this friend's car in Tehran. He is almost a generation older than Helali and his generation of *heya'ati* youth. He volunteered and went to war at fifteen, and he remembers how he used to revere Ayatollah Khomeini. Today, he would rather relax to Armstrong singing 'Love me tonight' than enter into the intensity of a Hosseinieh; he says he has difficulty believing the boy who would have given his life for Khomeini and the revolution was himself. This veteran's approach to 'bending the tools of militarism' differs from that of Helali's fans,

---

2 Ayatollah Khomeini ordered the establishment of the 'Organization for Mobilization of the Oppressed' (*Sazman-e Basij-e Mostaz'afin*) in 1979 and, with the outbreak of the Iran–Iraq war in 1980, called on its members to volunteer to fight.

82   *Sarah Walker*

but he shares with them a desire for a pleasurable form of lyricism and for the retrieval of something valuable from the rubble of Iran's history. In the words of popular *nohes*, 'everyone has a tranquil song' under Iran's 'bruised sky'.

References

Beeman, W. O. (2007). Music in a time of war: Response to papers presented for 'Musical Revolution, Revolutionary Music: Music and Conflict in the Persianate World', Society for EtÛomusicology Annual Meeting, Columbus.

Benjamin, W. (1992). Theses on the Philosophy of History. *Illuminations*. Trans. Harry ZoÛ. London: Fontana Press.

Benjamin, W. (1999). A Berlin Chronicle. *Selected Writings, Volume 2, 1927–1934*. Jennings, M. W., Eiland, H. and Smith, G. (Eds). Trans. Livingstone, R. *et al.* Cambridge, Mass. and London: The Belknap Press of Harvard UP.

Deghati, S. (2009). The Scent of Martyrdom. *Tehran Avenue*, www.tehranavenue.com/article.php?id=896 (accessed 19 July 2009).

Ellison, R. (1952). *Invisible Man*. New York: Random House.

Hirsch, M. (2001). Surviving Images: Holocaust Photographs and the Work of Postmemory. *The Yale Journal of Criticism, 14*(1), 5–37.

Razaf, A. (lyrics), Waller, T. 'Fats' and Brooks, H. (music) (1929). What did I do to be so black and blue? Santly Brothers, Inc., renewed by Chappell & Co., Inc.

Saeedi, S. (2009). Engineering Happiness. *Tehran Avenue*, www.tehranavenue.com/article.php?id=911 (accessed 31 August 2009).

8 Restoring Songs
On Mourning and an 'Everyday' Performance Genre in Northern Australia

Sally Treloyn

Introduction

Death and mourning have long been a focus of anthropological research motivated by the task of understanding the diverse social and cultural contexts in which people in the world conceive of their lives (Burbank *et al.*, 2008, p. 3). A preoccupation in the nineteenth and early twentieth centuries with death and mourning in Aboriginal Australian societies (Berndt, 1950; Kaberry, 1935; Mjöberg, 2012 (1915); Morphy, 1984; Spencer & Gillen, 1899) continues today extending across multiple disciplines including ethnomusicology, linguistics and research into Aboriginal and Torres Strait Islander health and wellbeing. Aboriginal communities experience some of the highest rates of death by preventable causes across generations in Australia, and amongst the highest in the world (Burbank *et al.*, 2008). Grief and loss are also felt in the wake of the forced removal of children from their families that occurred in Australia throughout part of the twentieth century (Atkinson, 2002), as well as high rates of attrition of linguistic and musical knowledges (Marett, 2010; Marett & Barwick, 2003). Insofar as grief and loss permeate multiple arenas of personal, social and cultural experience on a daily basis, research that seeks to better understand these experiences has never been more relevant.

Since songs, singing and dancing play a key role in ceremonies that accompany burial and mourning in many Aboriginal Australian life-worlds, substantial research conducted in northern Australia has touched on music. Most notable amongst ethnomusicological literature, Fiona Magowan has examined the role of Yolngu women's keening songs in mourning in northeast Arnhem Land (Magowan, 2007). Further to the west, Allan Marett has provided a seminal study of Wangga songs of the Daly-Fitzmaurice region, used in Kapuk 'Ragburning' mortuary ceremonies to facilitate the transition from life to death (Marett, 2000, 2002, 2005). Substantial earlier research has also documented and examined the role of music in various stages of mourning and burial, including: Stephen Wild's examination (with Margaret Clunies Ross) of Manikay and Bunggurl in the Larrgan stage of mortuary rites in northcentral Arnhem Land (Ross & Wild, 1984); Alice Moyle's recordings of songs from the Lardil Djawala mortuary ceremonial series sung following burial (Moyle, 1977, pp. 8–9); and Alice Moyle's recording of a

84   Sally Treloyn

women's 'Crying' song performed by a solo female singer (Okundjain (Kunjen)) in Wrotham Park that is usually performed 'at times of death and mourning' (Ibid., pp. 9–10) and of a song identified as Wu-ungka 'associated with death and mourning' performed by two women (Wikngatara (Wikalkan)) in Aurakun (Ibid., p. 14) in north Queensland.[1]

In the northwest of the continent in the northern Kimberley region, there is little to no evidence that singing and dancing have traditionally been used in formal ceremony surrounding death, burial and mourning, or at least in those parts of ceremony that have been witnessed by or described to anthropologists and other researchers. No mention of burial or mourning songs is made in Alice Moyle's survey of Kimberley music (Moyle, 1981). There is also no reference to song made in early anthropological descriptions of mortuary ceremonies in the region, including J. R. B. Love's substantial account of burial in the region of Kunmunya in the northwest (Love, 1936) or Phyllis Kaberry's discussion of mourning ceremonies amongst Kwini in the northeast (Kaberry, 1935). Anthony Redmond provides detailed descriptions and analysis of both Christian and original funeral practices amongst Ngarinyin in the Mowanjum Community and to the northeast, based on fieldwork conducted in 1995–2000 and discussions with senior elders born in the 1920s to 1930s and their descendents (Redmond, 2001a; 2008). The absence of references to song and singing in his accounts of original funeral practices, together with conversations that I have had with senior people in the region, suggest that there may in fact be no special ceremonial genre of song used exclusively to negotiate death and burials in the northern Kimberley. While contemporary Christian-format funerals feature hymns and other contemporary-style songs selected and/or performed by particular relatives of the deceased, sometimes played through loudspeakers, in many ways original funeral ceremonies around burial in this region are powerfully silent, punctuated only by wailing and ceremonial vocalisations (see Love, 1936; Redmond, 2008).

Why this is the case is not clear. Christian and Government ideologies from the 1920s restricted mortuary practices in the region, imposing Christian-style funerals on Aboriginal peoples. It is possible that, when they did occur, this imposition also had the effect of silencing them. It is not the purpose of this chapter to speculate on how this may be the case or to compare northern Kimberley practices with those elsewhere in the region or beyond. Rather, insofar as grief and loss permeate both ceremonial and non-ceremonial life in the contemporary worlds of Aboriginal communities in the region, it is important to look not only to performance genres that may have been used explicitly and traditionally in mourning and mortuary practices, but also to those that are used in day-to-day life. These include hymns, gospel, country and western, rock, hip hop and so on, that are

---

1 Elizabeth Mackinlay and John Bradley also note various genres and series used in the context of death and mourning in Yanyuwa community in the Gulf of Carpenteria (Bradley & Mackinlay, 2000; Mackinlay, 2005).

composed, performed and listened to, in order to express and negotiate intense and frequent experiences of death, grief and loss, along with a range of other emotions. In addition to contemporary styles such as these, attention also ought to be paid to everyday 'traditional' musical genres (i.e., genres used for celebration and entertainment and not explicitly for a ceremonial purpose) and styles that, while not used exclusively in mortuary ceremonies, play a clear role in negotiating loss and transitions between life and death. This chapter will turn attention to one such genre that is used to celebrate and reinforce community, family and personal identities at public festivals and other occasions: Junba, also referred to as 'Culture' or 'Corroboree'.

Referring to fieldwork conducted between 2000–2002 and 2010–2014 with mostly Ngarinyin peoples based in the town of Derby in the western Kimberley, and Communities of Mowanjum, Imintji, Kupungarri and Dodnun in the northern Kimberley, this chapter will consider the role that Junba plays in mourning, negotiating life and death, and mediating grief in a community of peoples where the loss of family is dealt with on a frequent basis.[2] Redmond has considered ways in which Ngarinyin personhood is 'distributed' (Redmond, 2008, 78), 'scattered' (Redmond, 2001a, Chapter 4), 'contained' (Redmond, 2001a, Chapters 4 and 6), and 'restore[d]' (Redmond, 2008, pp. 75, 80, 82) in social relationships with Country (places with which individuals and families trace ancestral and hereditary ties), kin and spirits. While he is careful to point out that Ngarinyin people do not necessarily experience loss more intensely than others, due to the distributed nature of the self in kin and Country, the loss of a person is experienced in culturally-specific and intensely psychophysical and psychosocial ways. Loss is negotiated by restoring the mourner through personal and social actions that 'value the co-inherence of self in [an] other' (Redmond, 2008, p. 83 fn14), and the self in past, present and future kin, and in Country.

This chapter will consider elements of the conception, composition, performance and transmission of Junba, to demonstrate ways in which this everyday, public, celebration-orientated genre brings to the fore and may work to restore personal and social identities in the day-to-day lives of communities facing loss. First, it is necessary to outline the construction of personhood in the northern Kimberley in more detail.

Personhood, Loss and Restoration in the Northern Kimberley

In order to appreciate how Junba contributes to the negotiation of loss and restoration of the self, we first need to consider the way in which personhood is experienced in this specific social setting. While understandings of personhood in Ngarinyin communities are heterodox (Redmond, 2008, p. 74 fn4), beliefs that are historically indigenous to the region and that persist today centre on identification with spirits of various classes and with place or 'Country'.

---

2 A 2010 report finds that the region has the highest rates of suicide in Australia (Senate, 2010).

86 Sally Treloyn

Spirits and Country

There are several classes of spirit that are frequently referred to in the Ngarinyin lifeworld, (also shared by their close neighbours the Worrorra and Wunambal peoples), that are central to the conception, birth, life and death of people. Key to the conceptualisation of self and place are three types of spirit:

1 *Wanjina. Wanjina* are localised spirits that create the landscape in the *Lalarn* (a continuing 'Dreamtime'), leaving impressions of themselves on cave walls. People trace patrilineal ties to their personal, family *wanjina* and the *gura* (Country) and, more specifically, *dambun* (clan Country) in which it resides.

2 *Wunggurr.* In the body of Country lies a more ubiquitous spirit known as *wunggurr*, often manifesting as a King Python and a jelly-like substance that contains the creative and reproductive essence of all living things, including the land itself, animals and human beings. *Wunggurr* is particularly present in waterholes and places that contain a third type of spirit, known as *anguma* (singular) or *burrunguma* (plural).

3 *Anguma.* The *anguma* is an aspect of a person's spirit that precedes their birth and life in the world. They typically reside in *wunggurr* places, and are associated with a *wanjina*. The *anguma* springs from Country and lodges itself in potential parents or associates, usually via a dream and/or the fat of a fish or animal. The *wunggurr* place, *wanjina* and animal from which the *anguma* comes, and the manner in which they sprung from these elements of Country, endure as foundational elements of the living person's body, name and identity as they live their lives: they make up the 'totems' and kin- and Country-based identities of living people.

A person, beginning their life as an *anguma* springing from ancestral Country lives in, and then in death eventually reincorporates into the *wanjina* from which he or she was born, their bones (until relatively recent times) returned to the *wanjina* cave by family (Redmond 2008). The *anguma* of a person also continues after their life, splitting from the body and travelling via caves in which the bones of the body are placed and tunnels to a place known as Dulugun (Mowaljarlai & Malnic 1993). Dulugun is identified by elders as Champagny Island, located off the western coast of the Kimberley, as well as the dark silhouettes of the countryside that are seen in the west (*gularr*) during the setting of the sun.[3] Once separated from the body, *burrunguma* spirits feel intense *marrarri* (sadness or sorrow) for their living kin and Country (Lommel & Mowaljarlai, 1994), and visit them in dreams and with the assistance of particular tidal currents and breezes.

---

3 *Agula* (referred to as *juwarri* or *jimi*) spirits also emerge from the body of a deceased person, but these spirits are more malevolent than *burrunguma* and can also be responsible for tricking people, causing them to get lost or lose their minds, even leading them to death.

One's identity is bound in the *wanjina* and Country from which one's *anguma* springs, that both precede and follow one's life. This shared identity is marked by self-referentiality in kinship and when referring to one's *wanjina*, to be described below.

Restoration and Containment

Redmond describes an intensely relational mode of realising self and others in the northern Kimberley life-world in which the identities of people, kin and Country are transcorporeal and co-inherent.[4] The co-inherence of one's self, one's kin and one's *wanjina*, in life, is demonstrated by what Redmond describes as 'progressive incorporation' in self-referential, generation-merging naming practices:

> there is a progressive incorporation of the deceased into the spirit world by the names of the dead generations becoming assimilated to the names of *wanjina*. The father's father's generational level is recycled backwards and forwards; the son's sons bear their names forward and the father's fathers recursively become part of an eternal generation of *wanjina*. A specific social identity is retained up until the second ascending generation, and is occasionally recoverable from older people for the third, but beyond that the distinction between the world of ancestors and historical personages becomes very unclear. (Redmond, 2001a, p. 119)

The identity of a person is thus 'distributed', sometimes dangerously (Redmond, 2008, pp. 74, 76), across space and society via identifications with close and extended kin, in the Country and with the spirits to which they are attached. Losing a person – or indeed losing an important part of Country – may entail a significant loss of an integral part of one's self.

In some ways loss of the self in relation to others occurs from the moment of conception and loss is a part of the distributed human condition. In order to be conceived, the watery yet-to-be-born *anguma* spirit splits or springs from its ancestors and patrifilial Country. In splitting from Country it is distributed in its parents, awaiting birth. When a baby is born there is another split, as the baby moves from its mother both physically and relationally, taking the opposite moiety to that which she has: the *Amarlarr* 'Bone' child springs from an *Ornorr* 'Dust' mother, and vice versa, demonstrating a culturally distinctive mode of indirect matrilineality unusual in northern Australia (Redmond, 2001a, pp. 125–236). Maternal kin feel *marrarri* 'sorrow' for the baby, linked as it is to its deceased *abi* (father's father) (Ibid.).

In relation to the contemporary mourning context of Christian funerals, Redmond describes the psychophysical effects of the 'distributed self' on mourners, noting that when a person loses a family member – co-inherent in their own

---

4 Redmond writes: '[T]ranscorporealization is . . . seen in naming practices which impart to an infant the name of a deceased paternal great-aunt or great-uncle, one's *abi*. When telling stories about that senior person and the ancestral *wanjina* with which both senior and junior *abi* are identified, they are referred to as 'I'' (Redmond, 2008, p. 80).

88 *Sally Treloyn*

personhood and identity – they 'may experience very real states of disintegration' (Redmond, 2008, p. 74): in the presence of kin now deceased, the very body of the mourner is threatened. Relatives express ambivalent emotions, invoking in the same or juxtaposed statements close, affinal relationships and dependence, and abandonment. Bodily actions such as beating one's own head with rocks, and throwing the body to the ground, or sometimes on the coffin, are not uncommon (Redmond, 2008, 76).

In hand with the potential for disintegration through the loss of someone who is so core to one's own identity, there is a range of other contexts in which there occurs a 'containing' (Redmond, 2008) and restoring of the self in relation to others. Following the separation of birth, maternal kin massage and rub the body of a baby with animal fats (Redmond, 2001a, p. 263) reminiscent of the fat in which the *anguma* travelled from Country to the parent. Likewise, in death, maternal kin rub bones of the deceased with red ochre and fat, restoring and reanimating them (Redmond, 2008, p. 78). The baby is then wrapped and cradled in *wulun* (the bark of the paperbark tree), its skin a fleshy pink (Redmond, 2008, pp. 78–79). The bones of the deceased are similarly wrapped in *wulun*, bound with string, and returned to the cave, *wanjina* and their kin, from which the *anguma* of the person came.

In death, the identity of the person is 'restored'[5] or re-contained: bones are wrapped in a paperbark wallet, and interred in a cave in their patrifilial Country, rejoining the bones and spirits of preceding generations in the place from which they were born and the *wanjina* that *is* them (Redmond, 2001a, pp. 133, 262):

> Grieving relatives participate in ceremonies which 'return' the individual subject to the ancestral realm, re-unifying that consciousness with the enduring *wanjina* ancestor and with what people call the 'eternal places' (as a gloss for *larlan* which can be understood as 'places which can be returned to'). It is this stratified entity which endures as various reincarnations of the ancestral being . . . (Redmond, 2001a, p. 263)

Through life, people ideally return to their Country, retouching, restoring or 'brightening' the *wanjina* from which they come (Blundell & Woolagoodja, 2005) and with which they will re-merge in death. In contemporary funeral contexts, mourners cite kin relationships with the deceased and attempt to rejoin the body of the deceased through the skin of the coffin, attempting to contain and restore the self.

Being born, living and dying entails a perpetuating pattern of splitting of the self from another, followed by restoration of the self via containment and reunification in relation to others. Distribution of the self, through identification with others and

---

5 Redmond cites Schutz and Luckman's (1974) idea of a quality of 'restorability' (Redmond, 2001a).

with place, and through restoration are inevitable or 'inescapable' processes in the Ngarinyin world (Redmond 2008, 83). These processes are key to negotiating life, death and loss in life. In the second part of this chapter the ways in which the conception and performance of Junba dance-song enact these processes and provide a performative framework to restore personal and community identities in relation to kin and Country in the context of community celebration, commemoration and pride, will be explored.

Junba: Restoring, Singing and Dancing

Junba is performed at public events in the Community of Mowanjum, Derby, elsewhere in the Kimberley, and further afield. It is indigenous to many of the 30-odd language groups of the Kimberley region, and is a cognate of Juju in the south and Nurlu and Ilma in the southwest (Glaskin, 2005, 2010, 2011a, 2011b; Keogh, 1990, 1995). Since at least the late 1990s, the primary context in which Junba has been performed is the annual festivals coordinated by the Mowanjum Art and Culture Centre and other town and community festivals. These festivals provide people with an opportunity to share and celebrate their particular Junba with neighbours and distant groups, following a tradition that predates the colonisation of the Kimberley region from the 1800s onwards. It is a dance-song genre in which children and adults of all ages can participate. Cultural heritage owners welcome visiting groups, who may receive the Junba being performed according to the Wurnan system of sharing, as well as visiting tourists who participate by watching, learning and listening.

While Junba is not explicitly linked to the formal ceremonies surrounding either original or modern burial styles, it plays an important role in the social and personal mediation of loss. For example, during the three-days of a 'bush' burial described by Redmond (at which I was also present), Junba (along with Wangga) was performed on two of the three nights. On other occasions, audio and video recordings of Junba have been used during a funeral and a wake, with copies distributed to family members of the deceased. In two recent Mowanjum Festival performances, lead *manambarra* (law people) have conducted *jolmon* 'serious talk' announcements, commemorating the lives and commenting on the significance of the loss of both senior and junior dancers before and during performances, marked by the striking of clapsticks and 'a minute's silence'. This practice also extended into collaborative presentations that I made with senior performers in the same period of time.

Underpinning these actions that link Junba and mourning is the way in which the conception of dance-songs, composition, performance and transmission encapsulates the patterns of containment and restoration that are core to personhood and negotiating loss in the day-to-day lives of the people who perform it. Selected instances of this in song conception and dancing, and the construction and performance of song texts, melody and rhythm will now be considered.

90 Sally Treloyn

Song-conception and Dancing

Various ways in which composers, dancers and singers reinvigorate relationships with deceased kin and Country in Junba dance-songs have been previously explored in some depth (Redmond, 2001a, 2001b; Treloyn, 2006a, 2006b). There are numerous accounts of the interaction between composers and *burrunguma* spirits (of deceased relatives) in dreams in which dances and songs are given to, witnessed by and imprinted or 'stuck' in the *ni* (mind) of the composer. This transaction involves a mutual, interdependent effort characterised by pulling and following (*biyobiyo*), and listening and learning (*dawul*) motivated by mutually felt sorrow (*marrarri*) and yearning, that both living and deceased kin act upon. Redmond describes how, when the experience of song-conception threatens the composer's psychic state, the body of the composer is touched and massaged by particular family members, restoring both connection with living kin and his physical integrity. Inasmuch as song-conception involves mutually felt emotion, effort and action, and restoring contact between the living composer, living kin, the kin that came before him, and the spirit underpinning all creativity in the world, song-conception demonstrates the notions of co-inherence and restoration, and mutually felt *marrarri* 'sorrow', in relation to kin and Country.

The gestures and choreographed actions of dancers also merge and co-inhere generations, people and Country on the dance ground. The archetypal Junba performance space comprises a screen constructed of wooden poles and branches (sometimes a canvas sheet) and an open, sandy space. Dancers prepare for each dance behind the screen and dance, with a stomping movement, from behind the screen across the open space towards the singing ensemble, which sits on the far side of the space fronted by the composer. The dancers enact exactly what the composer witnessed in his song-conceiving dream: they dance as the *burrunguma* – the spirits of the deceased family members – that he encountered and that danced for him. In coming from the screen, they come from Dulugun, just as the *burrunguma* in the composer's dream did, moving towards their living kin and Country. Insofar as the dancers are part of the composer's own extended family, usually the generation or two generations younger than him, he sees his grandparents (in his dream) move towards him in the bodies and actions of his grandchildren, echoing the generation-merging that characterises naming and kinship in Ngarinyin society.

In Jadmi-style Junba the dancers wear tall conical paperbark headcaps called *ngadarri*. As has been described elsewhere (Redmond, 2001a; Treloyn, 2006a), the paperbark headcaps function as the fleshy, paperbark wrappings of the bones of deceased family members, and of babies. Like the wrappings of babies and bones, the heads of the dancers are contained. Their bodies are painted, according to their moiety, in red ochre symbolic of dust (red earth) and white ochre (said to be fatty and deposited in the earth by *wunggurr*). Like *wanjina* in caves, babies and bones, bodies are restored and brightened on the dance ground, in relation to their kin and Country.

Dancing also invokes a 'merging' of living person with ancestral beings, be they moiety heroes (Wodoi, the spotted nightjar; Jun.gun, the owlet nightjar),

Restoring Songs 91

other animals, or ancestral famous historical figures, *agula* spirits, or *wanjina*. In Jerregorl style Junba the dancers carry large rounded boards (*balmara*), painted with images of *wanjina*, places or other ancestral beings. They are held behind the dancers' backs, their heads protruding from a small gap in the centre of the board. As Redmond has so evocatively described, the dancers, like *wanjina*, move Country as they move over the dance ground (Redmond, 2001b). Men and boys dance with the boards on their shoulders, tilting and swaying, and, in doing so, demonstrate and reinforce their relationships with deceased family members, the *wanjina*, and Country that they share.

Texts

Each song in a repertory has a unique text. This is relatively short and repeats cyclically throughout the course of the song performance. The origin, semantics and poetics of songtexts also invoke co-inherent and merged relationships between living dancers and Country, and the kin that both precede and follow them.

There are numerous instances of living composers and singers attributing the composition and content of lyrics to spirits in northern Australia, particularly in areas of the Daly-Fitzmaurice and Western Arnhem Land regions (Apted, 2010; Garde, 2005, 2007; Marett, 2000, 2005; O'Keeffe, 2010). In the case of Junba, a large number of songs describe the actions, motivations and feelings, and contain the words and utterances of *burrunguma*, which the composer saw and heard in his dreams. The words themselves are said to have been sung by *burrunguma* in the composer's song conception dream. The following text (one verse of a larger series of at least 34 verses) – composed by Ngarinyin/Wunambal composer Scotty Nyalgodi Martin in 1973 – refers to a *biyobiyo* or 'pulling and following' tension that, via a magic, deadly, radar-like cord known as a *buyu*, connects the composer to the *anguma* spirits, guiding him safely to witness songs and the Country to which they refer.

In singing these words, the composer is bringing the thoughts, feelings and experiences of his deceased family to life. His voice and those of his family accompanying him merge with those of family that has come before.

While the text refers to the interaction between a spirit and the composer, it also refers to the interaction between two spirits – one old and one young. In the dance accompanying this song, a fishing line, representing the *buyu*, is tied from the bough screen (from which spirits come) and stretched to the composer, sitting on the opposite side of the dance ground, at the front of the singing group. Two spirits – one old and one young – emerge from the screen, following the *buyu* with

Text:	*buyu minya redbendinga* x2	*biyobiyo memmurangi* x2
Gloss:	'this buyu, you pull'	'you follow this'

Figure 8.1 Buyu: song and gloss by Scotty Nyalgodi Martin, c.1973 (Barwick & Martin, 2003b)

92   *Sally Treloyn*

their hands in the darkness. In doing so, they emerge from a cave, where their bones reside, and which also serves as a tunnel entry to Dulugun (the island of the dead). Scotty Martin's son, Matthew Dembal Martin, an expert dancer of the 'young spirit' role, explains:

> The old man, he too old, he can't see that *buyu*, too old. 'I'm a . . . young man, I'll go front. You follow me. *Biyobiyo* [follow], *biyobiyo* behind'. That old man get it off me again: 'Where you going? What you going back for?', he tell me. 'Nah, come this way, come back', I'm bin pulling him back. (Personal communication, Matthew Martin and Sally Treloyn, Mowanjum, 6 December 2012)

In order to appreciate the power of song texts to restore the identity of living performers through interaction or the strengthening of ties with deceased family and Country, we also need to turn to the poetic techniques that are used in the construction of song texts. Insofar as all song texts consist of lyrics that were sung by spirits for the composer, all songtexts, sung from the throats (*langgan*) of living people, involve a merging of voices. In the song set out in Figure 8.1, for example, the identity of the speaker is typically ambiguous: it is the spirit speaking, it is Matthew thinking, and it is his father (Scotty) singing. Likewise, it is Matthew's father's grandfather's bones (the person who gave him the song) and his own body that move from the Dulugun cave behind the screen towards the living world of shared kin. There is an obfuscation of meaning and the identity of the speaker, which may contribute to the merging of identities. The conception and performance of the text co-inheres one generation in another: the living in the deceased and the deceased in the living.

Another key poetic technique that contributes to this merging of voices and identities is juxtaposition of minimally contrastive subjects – or parataxis – in the construction of song texts (Treloyn, 2007a). As in Figure 8.1, almost all Junba song texts comprise two different lines of text. Many texts have contrastive subjects in the A and B text-lines, be they distinct places, a person and an ancestral being, a person and an animal, an item of dance paraphernalia and an animal, and so on. The link between the two subjects in each text is rarely clear to uninformed listeners, however juxtaposition and parallel treatment (both syntactic and rhythmic) of the subjects draws them together. As Barwick has described in relation to Warumungu songs of central Australia in the Yawulyu song tradition, parallel treatment of otherwise paratactic song subjects in the two distinct text lines of a song 'invites consideration of . . . connection or equivalence' (Barwick, 2005, p. 14). An 'inductive space' (Ibid.) is formed on the dance ground, as one subject is seen and, in some cases, perhaps heard (Treloyn, 2007a) in relation to the other. While there is no explicit link provided in the text between the subjects we are invited to see the presence of one in the other. The dancers, singers and places, and ancestral beings named in the texts, co-inhere on the dance ground through dance, as well as through the semantic content and poetic construction of texts.

Restoring Songs 93

Melodic Setting of Texts: Text as a Body

Finally, as is common in Centralian-style song performance, Junba texts are performed isorhythmically – that is, each time the text is repeated it has an identical rhythmic setting: there is a strong, repeated association between a text and its rhythmic setting. Also, as is common in Centralian-style song performance, a flexible melodic pattern that remains the same from song to song in a repertory is set to the rhythmicised text, expanding and contracting within and between songs to accommodate texts and text units of different lengths and structures. While such a metaphor has not been discussed with performers, the melodic setting of rhythmicised texts can be compared to the restorative anointment of bones, babies and the composer's body. That is, melody is associated with taste (*wulag*) and sorrow (*marrarri*) for lost kin and Country and, inasmuch, has some association with other substances that have similar qualities, including fat, and a particular variety of ochre (Treloyn, 2006a); rhythm is associated with bone (*ornorr*) (Treloyn & Martin, 2012, 2014). The *ornorr* bone involves performance of the text with a particular rhythmic setting by a group in strong rhythmic unison – *balangarra biyobiyo* (everybody pulling/following together). The *wulag* taste (the melody) of the lost kin and Country is then set to the *ornorr* bone (text/rhythm). While speculative and reliant on implicit musical knowledge, it might be said that, like babies, bones, the body of the composer and the bodies of dancers, the bone of the Junba – the rhythmicised text – is rubbed/restored/contained with fat – the melodic contour – of the Junba.

Conclusion

Much of the previous discussion of the relationship between music and mourning in Australian Aboriginal societies has focused on the use of music in mortuary ceremonies, due to the prominent role that musical practices play in these contexts in many regions. In parts of the Kimberley where this is not the case, whether it be for cultural reasons or historical interventions, public 'everyday' dance-song genres such as Junba also play an important role in restoring people and communities in the wake of loss.

Singing and dancing Junba can lead to a restoration of the emotional and physical wellbeing of people (see Martin, in Treloyn & Martin 2014). Likewise, the wellbeing and 'abundant vitality' (Redmond, 2001a, pp. 230–231) of Country, made sad by the absence of the right people (ibid.), may also be restored (see Martin, in Treloyn & Martin 2014). Stories about the conception of Junba, song lyrics and dances all refer to interactions between living people, deceased kin and Country: songs come from ghosts, dancers dance as ghosts, singers sing the words of ghosts, and listeners listen to the words, thoughts and emotions of ghosts. Each of these performed transactions emphasises the mutually felt *marrarri* or 'sorrow' felt by both living and deceased kin, for one another.

The physical body and identity of the individual is restored through rubbing, containing and naming after the *anguma* splits from Country and the baby splits from parents in birth. Likewise the *anguma* spirit and bones split from the body in

94   *Sally Treloyn*

death and are recontained, rubbed and named in relation to the *wanjina* spirit and generations of kin that precede the deceased. Similarly the bodies of the composer and dancers are restored through touch and contact with kin, and the text/rhythm 'bone' of the Junba is revitalised when set with melody. Insofar as preceding and yet to be born generations and Country are central to Ngarinyin personhood, the ways in which people, spirits and Country are merged and co-presenced through Junba (via dance, song and the aesthetics, poetics, construction and melodic performance of song texts) reinforce or restore the identities of people. Singing and dancing Junba co-inhere the identities of people across generations, their deceased family, Country and *wanjina* spirits.

Everyday genres such as Junba are, in these ways, central to restoring the psychophysical wellbeing of people and of Country in the wake of losses: the day to day losses that are intrinsic to the experience of a person whose identity is 'distributed' amongst kin and in Country and in the tragic losses of elders, young people and children. Speaking of the containing and restoring processes of mortuary practices, Redmond has explained that:

> Maintaining the co-constitutive role of significant others within the self in this way may prevent a catastrophic collapse of the bereaved subject in a social milieu where people frankly acknowledge the inescapability of such processes. (Redmond, 2008, p. 83)

Junba, understood in the manner presented in this chapter, also serves as a preventative tool, practised in the everyday lives of people to manage and negotiate the devastating consequences of loss. Insofar as the Junba tradition itself is endangered, appreciating this has never been so critical.

References

Apted, M. E. (2010). Songs from the Inyjalarrku: the use of a non-translatable spirit language in a song set from North-West Arnhem Land, Australia. *Australian Journal of Linguistics, 30*(1), 93–103.

Atkinson, J. (2002). *Trauma trails, recreating song lines: the transgenerational effects of trauma in indigenous Australia*. North Melbourne, Vic.: Spinifex Press.

Barwick, L. (2005). Performance, Aesthetics, Experience: Thoughts on Yawulyu Mungamunga Songs. In E. Mackinlay, D. Collins & S. Owens (Eds.), *Aesthetics and Experience in Music Performance* (pp. 1–18). Newcastle, UK: Cambridge Scholars Publishing.

Barwick, L., & Martin, S. (2003b). Jadmi Junba by Nyalgodi Scotty Martin, Traditional Songman of the Dreamtime [Compact Disc and Notes]. Sydney: Rouseabout Records RRR135.

Berndt, C. H. (1950). Expressions of grief among Aboriginal women. *Oceania, 20*(4), 286–332.

Blundell, V., & Woolagoodja, D. (2005). *Keeping the Wanjinas fresh: Sam Woolagoodja and the enduring power of Lalai*. WA: Fremantle Arts Centre.

Bradley, J. J., & Mackinlay, E. (2000). Songs from a plastic water rat: An introduction to the musical traditions of the Yanyuwa community of the southwest Gulf of Carpentaria. *Ngulaig, 17*, 1–45.

Burbank, V., Glaskin, K., Tonkinson, M., & Musharbash, Y. (2008). Indigenous Ways of Death in Australia. In K. Glaskin, M. Tonkinson, Y. Musharbash, & V. Burbank (Eds.), *Mortality, Mourning and Mortuary Practices in Indigenous Australia* (pp. 1–20). Surrey, VT: Ashgate.

Garde, M. (2005). The Language of Kun-horrk in Western Arnhem Land. *Musicology Australia, 28*(1), 59–89.

Garde, M. (2007). Morrdjdjanjno Ngan-marnbom Story Nakka, 'Songs that Turn Me into a Story Teller': The Morrdjdjanjno of Western Arnhem Land. *Australian Aboriginal Studies, 2*, 35–45.

Glaskin, K. (2005). Innovation and ancestral revelation: The case of dreams. *Journal of the Royal Anthropological Institute, 11*(2), 297–314.

Glaskin, K. (2010). On dreams, innovation and the emerging genre of the individual artist. *Anthropological Forum, 20*(3), 251–267.

Glaskin, K. (2011a). Dreaming in Thread. In V. Strange & M. Busse (Eds.), *Ownership and Appropriation* (pp. 87–104). Oxford and New York: Berg.

Glaskin, K. (2011b). Dreams, memory, and the ancestors: creativity, culture, and the science of sleep. *Journal of the Royal Anthropological Institute, 17*(1), 44–62.

Kaberry, P. M. (1935). Death and deferred mourning ceremonies in the Forrest River tribes, North-West Australia. *Oceania, 6*(1), 33–47.

Keogh, R. (1990). *Nurlu songs of the west Kimberleys.* PhD diss. University of Sydney.

Keogh, R. (1995). Process models for the analysis of Nurlu songs from the western Kimberleys. In L. Barwick, A. Marett & G. Tunstill (Eds.), *The Essence of Singing and the Substance of Song: recent responses to the aboriginal performing arts and other essays in honour of Catherine Ellis* (pp. 39–51). Sydney: Oceania, University of Sydney.

Lommel, A., & Mowaljarlai, D. (1994). Shamanism in northwest Australia. *Oceania, 64*(4), 277–287.

Love, J. R. B. (1936). *Stone Age Bushmen of Today: life and adventure among a tribe of savages in north-western Australia.* London: Blackie.

Mackinlay, E. (2005). 'For Our Mother's Song We Sing': Yanyuwa Aboriginal Women's Narratives of Experience, Memory and Emotion. *Altitude, 6*, 1–10.

Magowan, F. (2007). *Melodies of Mourning: Music and emotion in Northern Australia.* Oxford: James Currey.

Marett, A. (2000). Ghostly voices: some observations on song-creation, ceremony and being in NW Australia. *Oceania, 71*(1), 18–29.

Marett, A. (2002). The Tide has Gone Out on Him. *Cultural Survival Quarterly, 26*(2), 22–25.

Marett, A. (2005). *Songs, dreamings, and ghosts: the Wangga of North Australia.* Middletown, CT: Wesleyan University Press.

Marett, A. (2010). Vanishing Songs: How Musical Extinctions Threaten the Planet. *Ethnomusicology Forum, 19*(2), 249–262.

Marett, A., & Barwick, L. (2003). Endangered songs and endangered languages. In J. Blythe & R. M. Brown (Eds.), *Maintaining the Links: Language Identity and the Land* (pp. 144–151). Bath, UK: Foundation for Endangered Languages.

Mjöberg, E. (2012 (1915)). *Among Wild Animals and People in Australia (Bland Vilda Djur och Folk I Australien).* Trans. M. Luotsinen & K. Akerman. Carlisle, WA: Hesperian Press.

Morphy, H. (1984). Journey to the Crocodile's Nest. Canberra: Aboriginal Studies Press.

Moyle, A. M. (1977). *Songs from North Queensland.* Canberra: Australian Institute of Aboriginal Studies.

Moyle, A. M. (1981). *Songs from the Kimberleys.* Canberra: Australian Institute of Aboriginal Studies.

96   Sally Treloyn

Mowaljarlai, D., & Malnic, J. (1993). Yorro Yorro: everything standing up alive: spirit of the Kimberley. WA: Magabala Books.

O'Keeffe, I. (2010). Kaddikkaddik ka-wokdjanganj 'Kaddikkaddik Spoke': Language and Music of the Kun-barlang Kaddikkaddik Songs from Western Arnhem Land. *Australian Journal of Linguistics, 30*(1), 35–51.

Redmond, A. (2001a). *Rulug Wayirri: Moving kin and country in the northern Kimberley.* PhD diss. University of Sydney.

Redmond, A. (2001b). Places that move. In A. Rumsey & J. F. Weiner (Eds.), *Emplaced myth: space, narrative, and knowledge in Aboriginal Australasia and Papua New Guinea* (pp. 120–138). Honolulu: University of Hawai'i Press.

Redmond, A. (2008). Time Wounds: Death, Grieving and Grievance in the Northern Kimberley. In K. Glaskin, M. Tonkinson, Y. Musharbash & V. Burbank (Eds.), *Mortality, Mourning and Mortuary Practices in Indigenous Australia* (pp. 69–86). Surrey, VT: Ashgate.

Ross, M. C., & Wild, S. A. (1984). Formal performance: the relations of music, text and dance in Arnhem Land clan songs. *Ethnomusicology, 28*(2), 209–235.

Senate, Community Affairs Reference Committee. (2010). *The hidden toll: suicide in Australia.* Canberra: Senate Printing Unit, Parliament House.

Spencer, B., & Gillen, F. J. (1899). *The Native Tribes of Central Australia.* London: Macmillan.

Treloyn, S. (2006a). *Songs that Pull: Jadmi junba from the Kimberley region of northwest Australia.* PhD diss. University of Sydney.

Treloyn, S. (2006b). Songs that Pull: Composition/Performance through Musical Analysis. *Context: Journal of Music Research, 31*, 151–164.

Treloyn, S. (2007a). Flesh with country: Juxtaposition and minimal contrast in the construction and melodic treatment of jadmi song texts. *Australian Aboriginal Studies, 2*, 90–99.

Treloyn, S., & Martin, M. D. (2012). *Australia's endangered song traditions.* Paper presented at the Music, Mind and Wellbeing Public Seminar Series. https://www.melbourn erecital.com.au/podcasts. Accessed 19 March 2013.

Treloyn, S., & Martin, M. D. (2014). Perspectives on dancing, singing and well-being from the Kimberley region of northwest Australia. *Journal for the Anthropological Study of Human Movement, 21*(1). http://jashm.press.illinois.edu/21.1/treloyn.html. Accessed 4 August 2014.

9 Music Therapy and Mourning

Katrina Skewes McFerran and Alexander Hew Dale Crooke

Music therapy is a profession that emerged in the post-World War II era in response to the identified needs of veterans who had been traumatised and injured by their experiences of war (Davis, Gfeller & Thaut, 2008). As such, the connection with mourning was established early and the role of professionals was to support individuals and groups to engage music in a way that addressed their health and wellbeing needs. The personal encounter between therapist and mourner has always been critical to this endeavour, since it allows them to discover together what kind of music will be most helpful in facilitating the grieving process. There are no assumptions that particular cultural traditions or musical stereotypes will be of benefit; instead, each mourner who elects to participate in music therapy has the opportunity to construct their own process, involving more, or less, music.

People who participate in music therapy frequently address issues of grief and loss associated with their other experiences of disability, mental and physical illness, or abuse. The age-old relationship between music and emotions makes this connection almost unavoidable. This chapter will focus specifically on times when music is used to facilitate the grieving process in response to the death of a close friend or relative. The example of adolescents will be used to illustrate this process, since young people provide particularly good examples of how existing relationships with music can be appropriated for healthy mourning. A research investigation of a school-based bereavement support group will illustrate the degree to which this is considered helpful by young people.

Music Therapy in Palliative Care

The use of music by therapists within palliative care contexts has been well documented and references to mourning are abundant in that context (Dileo & Loewy, 2005; Hilliard, 2005; Munro, 1984; Munro & Mount, 1978). Authors frequently describe working with patients as they prepare to die and the preparatory mourning that can be undertaken in anticipation of their own passing. Clare O'Callaghan (2013) describes how music can be used in legacy work with dying patients, generating messages and gifts for those who will be bereaved in the form of song compositions or compilations. Trygve Aasgaard (2001) describes a similar purpose in a children's hospital in Norway, but focuses on the ways that

98   Katrina Skewes McFerran and Alexander Hew Dale Crooke

songs contribute to building an ecology of love, where the life of the composed song continues to spread into the surrounding systems. Song writing is one of the most commonly documented strategies used by music therapists in the palliative care context (Daveson & Kennelly, 2000), and is usually described as relevant because it provides a medium through which both words and emotions can be simultaneously expressed and contained (Baker *et al.*, 2009).

The use of pre-composed songs can provide a similar vehicle for mourning within the palliative care context. Music therapists describe using songs for reminiscence (Hogan, 1999; Horne-Thompson & Grocke, 2008), again in preparation for an impending death. Denise Grocke (Grocke & Wigram, 2007) describes how songs facilitate access to existing memories and deepen existing relationships with others. In the field of music sociology, Tia DeNora (2000) describes how adults use personally significant songs in everyday life to frame experiences, allowing them to connect to the past and reintegrate different aspects of oneself in the current moment. More recently, music therapy scholars have expressed concerns that associating existing songs with loss and grief may sometimes exacerbate mourning, and some participants have described how the new meanings associating songs with grieving can powerfully trigger painful memories at unwanted times (Flynn, 2014). However, these kinds of unexpected associations may be unavoidable in the context of grieving and the benefits could be argued to outweigh the risks.

Some models of music therapy practice place greater emphasis on pure music making, preferring to avoid the specific meanings of words in favour of the possibilities of non-verbal domains. Improvisation has been introduced in this context by music therapists who facilitate anticipatory mourning processes, although this is less frequently described. Colin Lee (1995) and Nigel Hartley (1999) have described their work in the Creative Music Therapy tradition, using dyadic improvisations to communicate intimately with patients who are preparing for dying. Ruth Bright (2002) has described more structured use of music improvisations in mourning, illustrating an 'empty chair technique' for the client to symbolically express their feelings to the person whom they are grieving in order to release repressed emotions. In each of these examples, the therapists adopt a psychodynamic understanding of the music as a vehicle for projection of sub-conscious thoughts and feelings. This is distinct from the previous examples where the meanings made are more explicit and intentional and are related directly to mourning.

Music, Emotions and Teenagers

Young people have always made more time for music in their lives than adults, and by simple calculation their relationship with music is even more powerful. Studies consistently reveal that young people listen to between 2 and 3 hours of music per day on average (McFerran *et al.*, 2014; Miranda *et al.*, 2012; North & Hargreaves, 2000), and this number has remained remarkably stable despite the increasing use of music as part of technological multi-tasking along with gaming or social networking. Young people freely describe associating songs with emotions and moods, using music both intentionally and unintentionally as a soundtrack to their day (Miranda & Gaudreau, 2011; Saarikallio & Erkkila, 2007). The appropriation of known songs by young people as part of their mourning process is therefore often very natural and integrated with a range of other functions such as asserting identity and peer group affiliation (Gold, Saarikallio & McFerran, 2010).

Some concerns have been raised about whether independent music listening is always helpful for vulnerable young people, such as those who are mourning. Research has shown that depressed persons may be more inclined to use music for rumination (Garrido & Schubert, 2013), and an investigation of this possibility revealed that some depressed young people were inclined to use music repetitively and in isolation without achieving a sense of relief (McFerran & Saarikallio, 2013). Although some pundits suggest that it is the type of music young people listen to that has the melancholic effect, a critical interpretive synthesis of the literature linking young people, music and depression revealed no evidence to support this view (McFerran, Garrido & Saarikallio, 2013). Nonetheless, the review did confirm Adrian North's proposal (North & Hargreaves, 2008) that vulnerable young people can be at greater risk of negative emotional outcomes from independent music listening.

Music Therapy and Mourning Teenagers

Although young people use music naturally and frequently to address issues such as mourning, these studies suggest that it would be presumptive to assume that vulnerable young people are always benefiting from their music strategies. Participation in music therapy is one way of providing support to young people in managing this potent relationship between music and emotions at times of vulnerability, and a meta-analysis of preventative approaches with bereaved teenagers ranked music therapy as 'the most successful' intervention for supporting bereaved youth (Schlaug et al., 2005). Two evidence-based studies were highlighted in this review, with the first measuring behaviour and grief symptoms before and after eight weeks of music therapy, and finding significant improvements in both measures as rated in the home environment (Hilliard, 2005). The same researcher then conducted a follow-up study comparing music therapy to a social work group as well as a control (Hilliard, 2007). The music therapy process underpinning this intervention was active music making in the form of improvisation and other instrumental play methods and behaviours improved significantly as a result of participation in both music therapy and social work, but only the music therapy group achieved significantly reduced grief related symptoms. A second study noted in the meta-analysis investigated a bereavement support group for teenagers using a song writing intervention over eight weeks (Dalton & Krout, 2005). The group addressed different grief-related topics through song writing each week and once again, noticeable improvements in grief processing were captured by the results of the study as compared to a wait-list control group whose status remained relatively unchanged.

A number of studies have been undertaken in Australia to better understand how music therapy can be helpful to bereaved teenagers using interviews to collect young people's opinions. In the first study of this topic (Skewes, 2001), bereaved teenagers described a number of factors that they believed were critical to the positive outcomes they experienced as a result of participation in a weekly music therapy group in their school setting. They perceived opportunities for both freedom and control as mutually existing within the group, fostered by free instrumental play that encouraged personal expression. Their existing relationship with music was also utilised within the group as they contributed different songs for discussion across the weeks, which they found helpful for both emotional expression and identity formation. In addition, more general qualities of acceptance and respect were also valued by all the young people, and the safety and understanding they received from both musical and discussion based group encounters made an impression.

A follow-up investigation (McFerran, Roberts & O'Grady, 2010) adopted a slightly different approach based on feedback from the initial study and emerging understandings of grief, loss and resilience. Whereas a psychodynamic approach had informed the first study, emphasising containment, safety and the importance of expressing and understanding feelings associated with the loss in order to promote unfettered development, the next study adopted a framework of empowerment and resilience as tools for prevention. A heavier emphasis was placed on the young people's existing musical resources, namely their relationship with music, and song writing was used as the primary intervention rather than free associating with musical improvisations. After conducting interviews and analysing the descriptive data, a humorous play-on-words that reflected the overall tone of the adolescent group was constructed that encapsulated the findings – these young people were 'dying' to express their grief (McFerran, 2010b, p. 22) and appreciated the fun and creative opportunities to do so. They described being 'bottled up' before the group, 'hiding away' their grief so that people wouldn't be disturbed by their angst. They described 'releasing my feelings' within the group and 'letting it all out' and resultantly, being able to 'move on', 'get over it' and 'let it go'. They said they 'felt better'.

The research described above suggests that young people find the process of music therapy valuable, and that measurable improvements have been captured. The support of a music therapist can address the concerns about vulnerable young people using music in ways that reinforce pathological responses to grief. However, music therapists also recognise that the vast majority of people in mourning do not require professional therapeutic support (Bonono, 2008; Neimeyer & Currier, 2008). Music therapists have increasingly adopted a resilience-oriented perspective in considering their role in supporting people to use music as part of their mourning process, and ecological models of bereavement support for teenagers are appropriate to this task. Ecological models are outward-facing (Stige *et al.*, 2010), rather than focusing on an intense exploration and re-experience of grief and mourning. Music therapy group facilitators therefore adopt a participatory orientation 'emphasizing the existing resources of the young person and are

Music Therapy and Mourning 101

focused on context rather than historical cause' (McFerran, 2010a, p. 217). In this way, young people are assisted to access and express emotions, explore connections between themselves and their networks, and recognise the normal and healthy aspects of their grieving process that might otherwise be misunderstood as abnormal – such as staying connected to the deceased through dreams, linking objects and even wanting to talk to the person who has died (Klass, Silveran & Nickman, 1996).

The following section describes an ecologically informed research project, hosted by a public secondary school in Australia, where the authors examined the process and outcomes for young mourners who elected to participate in a music therapy group. The group was part of a larger programme running in the school that aimed to build a flourishing musical culture that would serve to enhance connectedness through inclusive opportunities for participation in music activities (McFerran & Rickson, 2014). The wellbeing officer in the school requested a bereavement specific group as part of the whole-school approach and we chose to collect data via student interviews in order to address the questions: what are the self-reported benefits of a music therapy programme delivered to a group of bereaved students, and what were students' experiences of the programme?

Research Design and Method

Participants

The school wellbeing officer was familiar with a number of mourning students, and invited them to participate in the music therapy programme. Six students agreed, although one was absent on both days of data collection. Of the five students that participated, three were female, three were from Anglo-Celtic backgrounds, and two were from Arabic backgrounds. Student ages ranged between 13 and 16 years old.

The Programme

The music programme was run once a week for five weeks in a private group setting. Each session lasted approximately 50 minutes. The ecological approach adopted by the facilitator meant that a democratic ethos was established and collaborations were actively pursued through ongoing consultation with group members about music repertoire to be shared and music activities to be used. The programme content was broadly structured around the seasons of the year, starting with autumn and ending in summer, based on a counselling programme that the wellbeing coordinator was familiar with (Newell & Moss, 2011). Within sessions, students chose to participate in a range of activities, including: sharing their own preferred songs that connected them to the person they were mourning; playing on a range of melodic and percussion instruments to express specific feelings in sound and to process what the grief related feelings sounded like; writing songs that addressed key topics of interest to the group, with one song being recorded that discussed the emotions of mourning and their desire to feel happy again; using picture cards to communicate about their experience of mourning; and frequent discussions in which they told the story of their loss, as well as processed the various activities.

Data Collection

Interviews and surveys were used to collect self-report data about the programme. Interviews were conducted in the week following the programme, and used a semi-structured schedule. This schedule aimed to evaluate the delivery of the programme, and questions also invited responses regarding the impact of the programme on experiences of mourning. In responding to open-ended questions, students offered insights into how music was appropriated both within sessions and in their everyday life.

Data Analysis

Taking a 'hybrid approach' (Fereday & Muir-Cochrane, 2008), interview data were analysed using both deductive and inductive methods. Data categories related to a priori research goals were established first, including reported wellbeing benefits, and programme attributes reported to facilitate benefits. Interview transcripts were then analysed inductively to identify codes, chosen to represent 'important moments' (Fereday & Muir-Cochrane, 2008) or 'key statements' (McFerran & Grocke, 2007). Codes were allocated to predetermined data categories and further analysed to form themes. Themes represented the results for each category, and provided a distillation of both reported benefits, and the elements of the programme perceived as facilitating such benefits.

Results and Discussion

Reported wellbeing benefits

Dealing with bereavement

Wellbeing benefits reported during interviews related primarily to an increased ability to cope with loss. This included coping at a general or day-to-day level, such as increased confidence to deal with everyday problems, getting 'back on track', and help with sleep issues. One girl described it in the following way.

> [The programme] kinda cheered me up, because, on that day that we did it, I found out more information about my dad, and it made me really upset, but then when we had the group, it made me like feel it was ok, because its ok to cry, and all that stuff.

Music Therapy and Mourning   103

This suggests, upon receiving information that exacerbated her grief, this girl found immediate comfort in the group. Perceivably, this was because she could discuss the event, and express her emotional response in a supportive environment.

Emotions

Students also described an impact on their everyday emotions and feelings through reports the programme made them feel 'better', 'happy' or 'less angry'. Some students also suggested they had become better at understanding and regulating their mood and emotions through participating in the group. The latter is evident in one boy's response when asked if the programme had changed his relationship with music.

> Yeah, sort of. The songs like, they change your feelings, when you're feeling down you listen to music and you feel at least a bit better.

This response indicates the boy had not only learnt how to mitigate negative feelings, but had also become cognisant of how music could be appropriated to do so.

Remembering the Good Things

Participants reported that the programme had also helped them manage experiences of mourning connected to memory. This encompassed the ability to connect with good memories, as articulated in one boy's perception of song sharing, and the role of music more generally.

> It was good because, I remembered the song I used to sing with my mum [which] reminded me of the times that I used to have fun with my mum.

Another girl offered a similar statement when asked to give an overall description of the programme at the start of the interview.

> We talked about the Autumn, Summer, Spring and Winter. And Summer is to, like, finally move on and think of that person in happy ways, not sad ways.

This girl seems to be suggesting that remembering positive things about her loved one, rather than focusing on the 'sad' memories, was a central element of the programme.

Moving Forward

As in the above quotation, some students suggested the programme helped them to move on. One girl described this in the following way.

I was always upset about my dad passing away, and finally I have realised that like I don't have to cry all about the sad parts, I can just be happy that he's not in pain anymore, and I can think about happy parts.

This describes several aspects of 'moving forward'. First, a moving on from dwelling on 'sad' feelings, then an acceptance of what has happened, and finally the ability to focus on positive aspects of the relationship. It seems that the programme facilitated a progression through stages of mourning to a more positive position for this girl.

Reponses from other students suggested they had not moved on, yet the programme was beneficial in providing a forum for seeking advice and strategies to do so.

I could go to them and ask them any questions about 'Is it going to get easier?', 'When?', not when but like, 'Am I going to move forward soon or whatever?'

This suggests, even though this girl had not moved on, the ability to connect with others, and hear that she would eventually, was also valuable.

Social Connection

The opportunity to spend time with others experiencing bereavement was another reported benefit. While most students already knew each other, hearing each other's stories reportedly helped form deeper connections. For example, when asked if he had changed after participating in the programme, one boy made the following statement.

I've changed by . . . now I know the people even better, now we all know each other's stories.

This response, and others like it, implies the opportunity to share stories and connect through the programme formed deeper social connections between members.

Social Support

Students also described that the group supported them to form a social network that went beyond connection and sharing. One girl describes this when responding to the question of whether finding the time to participate was hard, or required any sacrifices.

Not really, I was just ready to go and tell what happened to my dad, and see about my friends, what they were in there for, see if I could help them with any advice.

She perceives the support within the group as reciprocal, and helping others by sharing about her own mourning was a factor that motivated this girl to attend sessions. Other quotations also indicate that this social support became self-sustaining.

Whenever you have like a bad problem, you always know that you have someone to go to, to express them, and there is always someone to tell. [It has helped] knowing that there is always somebody there to help you out.

That this girl describes someone 'always' being there suggests support transcended session boundaries, and extended into her social world.

Letting it Out

The opportunity for self-expression in the group was reported as another important outcome. When asked what she thought of the song writing process, one girl made the following statement.

[It was] pretty good, just to like, if I said there was something that I was feeling, it would be like letting everyone know how I was feeling at the time, or after losing mum.

Being able to express her feelings about losing her mother was seen here as a significant benefit for this girl. Further, the comment that 'it would be *like* letting everyone know' indicates the song writing process provided a non-confronting vehicle for this expression. The same girl went on to articulate the benefit of this expression.

Yep, I'm a lot happier after [. . .] letting all those feelings out.

The idea of 'letting them out' suggests these were thoughts or feelings that this girl had previously internalised, or kept to herself. That being able to give voice to, or express these feelings, led to this girl feeling 'a lot happier' indicates this was a cathartic process.

Aspects of the Music Programme Students Reported as Helpful

Student perceptions of how and when the programme helped facilitate the benefits reported above were also captured in interviews. These included the musical attributes of the programme as well as aspects of the group format such as setting and space.

The music

HOW MUSIC HELPED

In many cases students reported it was the music, or musical processes, that facilitated benefits. For example, when describing the 'best bit' of the programme, one boy explained the impact of song writing.

Doing the song at the end, because it was just fun. Both because it was fun, and because it helped me deal with problems.

This suggests that sometimes a safe setting for expression and grappling with mourning was provided within, or through, the music itself. Another participant also cited the song writing process as beneficial. After reporting she had changed as a result of her participation – she become happier through being able to talk to people and express her feelings to others – she was asked what role she thought music had played in this process:

> When we were writing the song, I got to say a lot about how I was feeling, and I got to hear how others were feeling, and how they found a way to move forward, and sort of get happier in life.

This was supported by other responses that specifically articulated the role of music as a vehicle for expression. For example, when asked what the role of music was in sharing her experiences, one girl made the following statement.

> It just like helps you express your feelings a lot easier [. . .] if you're confused, there's music for that, or if you're sad, there's music for that, or happy or anything. There's always music to explain how you're feeling.

This response not only explains how music enabled students to express themselves, it also suggests that, through the programme, students learnt to appropriate music as a health resource.

CHANGE IN MUSICAL RELATIONSHIP

A number of the young people described how participation in the programme had helped them to appropriate music in new ways that changed their understandings of music. When asked if the programme had changed his relationship with music, one boy made the following statement.

> Yes it has, because, when we were in the group we've been talking about how music can help you get back on the right track, and yeah, it's really good.

One girl goes on to describe how this new relationship with music, exemplified here in terms of increased music listening, impacted her everyday life.

> [. . .] it keeps me calm when I'm really upset, or angry, it just keeps me relaxed. It helps me go to sleep some nights when I can't go to sleep. It just helps me through the day.

This suggests that helping young people learn about how to appropriate music listening as a resource in their daily lives can impact their wellbeing. Another student expressed how she came to understand that instruments could be used as a resource. She describes the role of drum improvisation as a vehicle for expression.

It was different to find out different ways of playing different feelings. I never thought that different sounds could mean different things. I used to just think they were sounds, but now I know that they can mean different things. [It helped because], if I wanted to get my feelings out, I could play the drums and play the feeling that I'm feeling.

The discussion of meaning here suggests gaining a deeper understanding of the potential of music for expressing emotions. Students also articulated their new relationship with music in terms of increased understanding of and appreciation for particular musical elements, including lyrical content and 'the different beats of the songs'. Others reported increasing awareness that music can help them concentrate in school, helping to counter the distraction that grieving promoted.

MUSICIANSHIP NOT REQUIRED

While students reported instrumental use as a helpful way of achieving benefits, prior experience or musical skill was not perceived as prerequisite. One student suggested that the fact they had never played drums did not impede the benefits they experienced from improvisation sessions. Another boy made the following statement.

[Drumming] was really fun . . . I really don't like drums, but because we did different beats, it was enjoyable. It helped with the programme because it got me back on track.

Using drums to express feelings rather than as the foundation for acquiring skills re-engaged this young man in music. Once the requirement of achieving expertise was removed, a lack of skills was no longer problematic. In this way, the therapeutic potential of an instrument can be made available to the least 'musically expert' students.

WE ALSO HAD FUN

Students consistently reported that having music in sessions made them fun. This fun appeared beneficial on multiple levels. It was reported to offer a less threatening way to address issues of mourning, and provide relief from the more challenging aspects of the programme. Sometimes this was described almost as a balancing act.

[. . .] we were trying to make a song that kinda-like brought back memories, but trying not to make it like really sad, trying to make it funny. And we got half way through, of making it sad and funny at the same time.

Here it appears this balance was important for the grieving process. While acknowledging the pain and sad memories was necessary for moving forward, it also seemed important not to dwell on these too much. It was possible to mourn and have fun within a single experience.

108   *Katrina Skewes McFerran and Alexander Hew Dale Crooke*

HARD BUT WORTH IT

Just as fun was a common theme of the programme, so too were the challenging aspects of participation. Processes such as sharing stories were reported as 'difficult', 'embarrassing', and 'very depressing' activities in which people 'cried a lot'. One student reported 'knowing you have to tell your story' made him apprehensive about attending some sessions. However, students also acknowledged these challenges were valuable.

> I was upset, but also kinda relieved that I could tell someone what I was going through.

This and similar quotations suggest it was often through difficult experiences that benefits were achieved. As such, it would seem these challenging experiences are a necessary element of programmes looking to address bereavement. Further, it appears music can provide a valuable medium through which a balance between challenging emotional processing and fun can be achieved.

Setting and Space

PRIVATE GROUP SETTING

When asked what the 'best bit' about participating in the programme was, one girl answered in the following way.

> Just listening to each other and knowing that it's confidential, they won't go out and blab or laugh at you because you cried about it, and we've all been through the same thing.

This suggests the private and confidential setting was important for this girl, and provided the safety and comfort necessary for her to express herself. The size of the group was also important. While two students suggested they would like to see bigger groups in the future, many reported the smaller group meant they got to know everyone better, which in turn led to increased trust, connection, commitment to the programme and social support between members. Small group size also meant all members were given the chance to have their say during sessions:

> [. . .] everybody had a chance to get involved, it wasn't always one person getting chosen, it was always, everybody had their option to have their say in whatever it was.

Having a say in 'whatever it was' was interpreted to mean all members were given a chance to both make decisions about the content and structure of the programme, as well as to share their experiences of bereavement.

GAVE US THE SPACE AND PLACE

Students also described how sessions provided a physical place and emotional space for connecting with others and expressing their feelings. For example, when asked why he chose to participate, one boy answered in the following way.

> Because normally I wouldn't have anyone to speak to about my feelings, and there was good friends that you can trust and won't say nothing to other people.

Interestingly, while this boy notes he already had 'good friends that you can trust', he also indicated before the programme he didn't have anyone to talk to about his feelings. This suggests the programme provided a place for these friends to come together in such a way that it formed a safe emotional space for them to share their feelings.

Conditional Outcomes

While the above results give an overwhelmingly positive account of how these young people appropriated music to support their mourning process with the support of a music therapist and wellbeing coordinator, there were some limitations. Some participants made comments that are worthy of note in understanding the extent of benefit. The following quotation provides an important reminder to anyone working with music in this area.

> I wasn't really coping well, [. . .] and I'm still not coping with it. [The music group] helped a lot, I'm not always depressed or upset about anything, about what happened to my dad, and it's just made me feel a bit happy.

While suggesting the programme was helpful, there are several important qualifications within this statement. First, the girl acknowledges that after the programme she is still not coping with the loss of her father. While not being 'always depressed' is an improvement, this suggests depression is still present. Such statements clarify that music should not be considered a panacea, nor music programmes expected to remove the pain of loss altogether. The fact that this girl did at least feel 'a bit happy', however, is not to be overlooked either. For someone mourning a significant loss on a daily basis, any reprieve can be a significant outcome.

Conclusions

A music therapy bereavement support group can be seen as a way of establishing a mourning ritual for young people in the context of contemporary school-based services. The form of the group ritual described in this chapter has been nuanced over time in response to feedback from participants in groups and emerging research findings in the field of loss and grief more broadly. Whilst initial adolescent bereavement support groups adopted a psychodynamic lens on the assumption that unresolved grief could lead to mental health problems, recent studies show that most people are able to successfully navigate their own mourning processes without professional support (Neimeyer & Currier, 2008). In addition, the return to typical levels of functioning following a significant bereavement can occur relatively quickly for those who are mentally stable prior to the loss (Bonono, 2008). The young people's reports on their experience of the most recent bereavement support group show that adopting a non-pathological, resilience-oriented approach was just as helpful and in similar ways to the initial orientation. Rather than relating their mourning to unconscious processes through music, the young people benefited from learning how to use music as a health resource whilst mourning.

Ensuring that young people appropriate music in ways that support their mourning processes is an important achievement. The literature suggests that music can be just as powerful in reinforcing unhelpful grieving behaviours such as rumination (Garrido & Schubert, 2013), particularly when the young person has a pre-existing struggle with depression (McFerran & Saarikallio, 2013). In addition, not all young people think about using music as a part of their grieving rituals, despite the statistics that suggest how important it is to many adolescents (Miranda, 2012). The young people in this study describe their experiences in both these areas. For some, it was the realisation that music can hold their emotions and support them in making meaning from their loss. For others, it was a greater consciousness that this requires intentional decisions.

What is also apparent in the reports of these young people is a growth in their uses of music with others, rather than in isolation. All the young people describe the sense of connectedness and support that was generated through sharing their stories and their music as a part of this mourning ritual. This has also been described in previous studies (McFerran, 2006) and requires more emphasis in the future. In many ways, this connectedness seems to be the most powerful and sustainable outcome from the music group. Music is able to bring people together in sharing their mourning, providing conditions that support emotional connections both internally and to others. This is particularly important to mourning youth, who are at risk of feeling isolated because of the existential crisis that accompanies mourning at a time when they are developmentally primed to be focused on being invincible.

The use of music as a part of mourning rituals is clearly relevant for young people although caring adults need to be alert to ensure that the strategies adopted by grieving youth are helpful. When used well, music fosters connections that support mourning by connecting to emotions, memories and others who understand. To embed this potential for connectedness within musical mourning rituals such as a bereavement support group creates the conditions most likely to be conducive for young people to grow in response to a significant loss.

References

Aasgaard, T. (2001). An ecology of love: Aspects of music therapy in the pediatric oncology environment. *Journal of Palliat Care, 17*, 177–181.

Baker, F., Wigram, T., Stott, D., & McFerran, K. S. (2009). Therapeutic songwriting in music therapy: Who are the therapists, who are the clients, and why is songwriting used? *Nordic Journal of Music Therapy, 18*(1), 32–56.

Bonono, G. A. (2008). Grief, trauma and resilience. *Grief Matters: The Australian Journal of Grief and Bereavement, 11*(1), 11–17.

Bright, R. (2002). *Supportive Eclectic Music Therapy for Grief and Loss: A Practical Handbook for Professionals*. St Louis: MMB Music Inc.

Dalton, T. A., & Krout, R. E. (2005). Development of the grief process scale through music therapy songwriting with bereaved adolescents. *The Arts in Psychotherapy, 32*, 131–143.

Daveson, B., & Kennelly, J. (2000). Music therapy in palliative care for hospitalised children and adolescents. *Journal of Palliative Care, 16*(1), 35–39.

Davis, W., Gfeller, K., & Thaut, M. (2008). *An introduction to music therapy : Theory and practice.* (3rd ed.). Silverspring, ML: American Music Therapy Association.

DeNora, T. (2000). *Music in everyday life*: Cambridge University Press.

Dileo, C., & Loewy, J. V. (Eds.). (2005). *Music therapy at the end of life*. Cherry Hill, NJ: Jeffrey Books.

Fereday, J., & Muir-Cochrane, E. (2008). Demonstrating rigor using thematic analysis: A hybrid approach of inductive and deductive coding and theme development. *International journal of qualitative methods, 5*(1), 80–92.

Flynn, L. (2014). *The stories we haven't told: The lived experience of music used in therapy for bereaved parents.* PhD diss., University of Queensland, Australia.

Garrido, S., & Schubert, E. (2013). Adaptive and maladaptive attraction to negative emotion in music. *Musicae Scientiae, 17*(2), 147–166.

Gold, C., Saarikallio, S., & McFerran, K. S. (2010). Music Therapy. In R. J. R. Levesque (Ed.), *Encyclopedia of Adolescence*. New York: Springer.

Grocke, D., & Wigram, T. (2007). *Receptive methods in music therapy: Techniques and clinical applications for music therapy clinicians, educators and students.* London, Philadelphia: Jessica Kingsley Publishers.

Hartley, N. (1999). Music therapists' personal reflections on working with those who are living with HIV/AIDS. In D. Aldridge (Ed.), *Music therapy in palliative care: New voices* (pp. 105–125). London: Jessica Kingsley Publishers.

Hilliard, R. E. (2005). *Hospice and palliative care music therapy: A guide to program development and clinical care*. Cherry Hill: Jeffrey Books.

Hilliard, R. E. (2007). The Effects of Orff-Based Music Therapy and Social Work Groups on Childhood Grief Symptoms and Behaviours. *Journal of Music Therapy, 44*(2), 123–138.

Hogan, B. (1999). The experience of music therap for terminally ill patients. In R. R. Pratt & D. Grocke (Eds.), *Music Medicine 3* (pp. 242–252). Melbourne: Faculty of Music, University of Melbourne.

Horne-Thompson, A., & Grocke, D. (2008). The effect of music therapy on anxiety in patients who are terminally ill. *Journal of Palliative Medicine, 11*, 582–590.

Klass, D., Silveran, P. R., & Nickman, S. L. (Eds.). (1996). *Continuing bonds: New understandings of grief*. Washington, DC: Taylor and Francis.

112   Katrina Skewes McFerran and Alexander Hew Dale Crooke

Lee, C. (1995). *Lonely waters: Proceedings of the International Conference, Music Therapy in Palliative Care*. Oxford: Sobell Publishers.

McFerran, K., Garrido, S., O'Grady, L., Grocke, D., & Sawyer, S. M. (2014). Examining the relationship between self-reported mood management and music preferences in Australian teenagers. *Nordic Journal of Music Therapy*. doi: 10.1080/08098131.2014.908942

McFerran, K., & Grocke, D. (2007). Understanding music therapy experiences through interviewing: A phenomenological microanalysis. *Microanalysis in music therapy*, 273–284.

McFerran, K. S. (2006). Tipping the Scales: Fostering a healthy adolescence through musical participation (pp. 25). Melbourne: University of Melbourne.

McFerran, K. S. (2010a). *Adolescents, Music and Music Therapy: Methods and Techniques for Clinicians, Educators and Students*. London: Jessica Kingsley Publishers.

McFerran, K. S. (2010b). Tipping the scales: A substantive theory on the value of group music therapy for supporting grieving teenagers. *Qualitative Inquiries in Music Therapy (A Monograph Series), 5*, 2–49.

McFerran, K. S., Garrido, S., & Saarikallio, S. (2013). A Critical Interpretive Synthesis of the literature linking music and adolescent depression. *Youth and Society, Online First*. doi: 10.1177/0044118X13501343

McFerran, K. S., & Rickson, D. J. (2014). Community Music Therapy in schools: Realigning with the needs of contemporary students, staff and systems. *International Journal of Community Music, 7*(1 Special Issue on Community Music Therapy), 75–92.

McFerran, K. S., Roberts, M., & O'Grady, L. (2010). Music therapy with bereaved teenagers: A mixed methods perspective. *Death Studies, 34*(6), 541–565.

McFerran, K. S., & Saarikallio, S. (2013). Depending on music to make me feel better: Who is responsible for the ways young people appropriate music for health benefits. *The Arts in Psychotherapy, 41*(1), 89–97.

Miranda, D. (2012). The role of music in adolescent development: Much more than the same old song. *International Journal of Adolescence and Youth, iFirst*, 1–18.

Miranda, D., & Gaudreau, P. (2011). Music listening and emotional well-being in adolescence: A person- and variable-oriented study. *European Review of Applied Psychology, 61*(1), 1–11.

Miranda, D., Gaudreau, P., Debrosse, R., Morizot, J., & Kirmayer, L. J. (2012). Music listening and mental health: Variations on internalizing psychopathology. In R. A. R. MacDonald, G. Kreutz & L. Mitchell (Eds.), *Music, Health and Wellbeing* (pp. 513–529). Oxford: Oxford University Press.

Munro, S. (1984). *Music therapy in palliative/hospice care*. St Louis: Magnamusic-Baton.

Munro, S., & Mount, B. M. (1978). Music therapy in palliative care. *Canadian Medical Association Journal, 119*, 1,029–1,034.

Neimeyer, R. A., & Currier, J., M. (2008). Bereavement interventions: Present status and future horizons. *Grief Matters: The Australian Journal of Grief and Bereavement, 11*(1), 18–22.

Newell, S., & Moss, A. (2011). *Supporting children and young people through change, loss and grief: an evaluation of the Seasons for Growth program*. Sydney: Southern Cross University.

North, A. C., & Hargreaves, D. J. (2000). The importance of music to adolescents. *British Journal of Educational Psychology, 70*, 255–272.

North, A. C., & Hargreaves, D. J. (2008). *The social and applied psychology of music*. New York: Oxford University Press.

O'Callaghan, C. C. (2013). Music therapy preloss care though legacy creation. *Progress in Palliative Care, 21*(2), 78–82.

Saarikallio, S., & Erkkila, J. (2007). The role of music in adolescents' mood regulation. *Psychology of Music, 35*(1), 88–109.

Schlaug, G., Norton, A., Overy, K., & Winner, E. (2005). Effects of music training on the child's brain and cognitive development. *Annals of New York Academy of Science, 1060*, 219–230.

Selfhout, M. H., Branje, S. J., ter Bogt, T. F. & Meeus, W.H. (2009). The role of music preferences in early adolescents' friendship formation and stability. *Journal of Adolescence, 32*(1), 95–107.

Skewes, K. (2001). *The experience of group music therapy for six bereaved adolescents.* University of Melbourne, Melbourne, Australia.

Stige, B., Ansdell, G., Elefant, C., & Pavlicevic, M. (2010). *Where music helps: Community music therapy in action and reflection.* Surrey, UK: Ashgate.

10 Embracing Life in the Face of Death

Community Singing with the Elderly

Jane W. Davidson

Introduction

The word 'grief' comes from a Latin word (via Old French) that means 'burden'. The *Oxford English Dictionary* Online (2012) defines it as 'mental pain, distress, or sorrow . . . Deep or violent sorrow, caused by loss or trouble; a keen or bitter feeling of regret for something lost, remorse for something done, or sorrow for mishap to oneself or others'. It is most often used in relation to the loss surrounding the death of a loved one. However, people with terminal illnesses or the elderly also experience grief in the face of their approaching loss of life. This is known as 'preparatory grief'.

Preparatory grief is defined as 'that [grief that] the terminally ill patient has to undergo in order to prepare himself for his final separation from this world' (Kubler-Ross, 1969, p. 76) It is experienced by virtually all patients who are facing the inevitability of their own death due to illness or advancing age, and can be facilitated with psychosocial support and counselling (Periyakoil & Hallenbeck, 2002). Persons who are dying may grieve the coming separation from loved ones as well as the simple pleasures of life they will lose. They may also mourn lost opportunities such as the chance to enjoy much anticipated events like the arrival of grandchildren (Periyakoil & Hallenbeck, 2002). The grief experienced may result in social withdrawal and detachment, reducing the patient's ability to do the emotional work of separating and saying goodbye, and causing anguish and worry in family members and friends (Mystakidou *et al.*, 2008).

With increasing infirmity due to age, elderly people also experience other significant losses such as that of their independence, way of life and self-image (Periyakoil & Hallenbeck, 2002). They may also mourn the changes to their physical and mental capacities and the resultant changes to their family roles (Mystakidou *et al.*, 2008). These losses necessitate periods of adjustment and grieving in order to be able to develop a new equilibrium in the face of the changed circumstances (Humphrey & Zimpfer, 2008). 'Mourning' is associated with the expression of such grief or sorrow. It can also be understood in broader terms as 'yearning; pining from love' or 'a conventional or ceremonial manifestation of grief for the death of a person' (*Oxford English Dictionary* Online, 2012). The elderly may also be in mourning for the loss of spouses and other relatives. Isolation, loneliness and deteriorating health

Embracing Life in the Face of Death 115

can place the elderly at risk for more complicated grief outcomes in such situations (Davidson & Fedele, 2011; Gilliland & Fleming, 1998).

Another type of grief is the grief experienced by people before the death of a loved one. Lindemann (1944) first coined the term 'anticipatory grief' to refer to the experience of people whose relatives had been sent to fight in the war but had not died. This has now expanded into a large body of research investigating the mourning that occurs in anticipation of the death of a loved one. The term can also apply to carers of the elderly or of dementia patients who witness the deterioration of health and eventual death of the person they care for.

Caring for a family member with dementia involves loss and inevitable grief throughout the duration of the illness. Emotional strain and significant levels of depression, burnout and decreased life satisfaction have been found to be associated with caregiving (Lindgren, Connelly & Gaspar, 1999). Of course, death of the care recipient is the ultimate loss, but grief as a reaction to non-death losses has also been found to be a part of the family caregiver's experience. Chronic illness produces continual, partial losses of the individual as a cognitive, functioning human being (Rando, 1986). Caregivers' grief may therefore stem from a loss of companionship with the afflicted as their functional abilities decrease, and other changes in the relationship with the afflicted person (Lindgren *et al.*, 1999). Carers also mourn the changes in their own lives associated with taking on the role of a caregiver (Duke, 1998).

Anticipatory grief is statistically similar to conventional grief on the majority of subscales on the Grief Experience Inventory, but is associated with more intense anger, loss of emotional control and complicated grief (Gilliland & Fleming, 1998). Lengthy chronic illnesses are particularly associated with complicated bereavement (Gerber *et al.*, 1975; Sanders, 1982). In one study, family caregivers described their pre-death grief as raw, overwhelming and wrenching (Collins *et al.*, 1993).

However, those who suffer anticipatory grief appear to report less acute symptoms of grief after bereavement, indicating that some benefit is obtained by the previous grief work undertaken (Gilliland & Fleming, 1998). It tends to foster closer ties to the person whose life is threatened and a desire to stay close to them (Parkes, 1998). Therefore, the facilitation of such grief work for carers of the elderly or ill is an important consideration.

Community music making as therapy and the current project

Music has a long association with ritualised behaviours around grief, with the discipline of music therapy having devised specialised techniques to assist in the ritualised behaviours. In such contexts, the therapeutic relationship between patient and therapist is explicit and the work undertaken is often challenging, though undoubtedly often highly positive for both parties. For example, Colin Lee (1996) and David Aldridge (1999) both charted the passage to death of professional musicians by working through a series of musical and personal farewells. In a far less explicitly therapeutic or ritualised format, there has been a considerable increase in

116 *Jane W. Davidson*

the promotion of structured singing groups offered for health and wellbeing. Such groups are often led by musicians without any formal training as therapists, with an emphasis being on obtaining the benefits inherent in group 'musicking' (Small, 1998). Sound Sense, a UK agency that promotes community music, defines it as a practice that 'involves musicians from any musical discipline working with people to develop active and creative participation in music . . . [It] helps people to make music – on their own terms.'[1] Recent community music therapy work has embraced new areas of application, including choirs for the elderly (Stige, Ansdell & Elefant, 2010).

The benefits of singing to wellbeing are well documented. Singing and musical activity are commonly referred to as 'non-pharmacological interventions' in the context of elderly care and dementia (MacKenzie, 2011). Daniel Levitin (2008) has identified six basic functions of song: knowledge, friendship, religion, joy, comfort and love. Ruud (2012) has also identified four dimensions or categories of quality of life that benefit from musicking: vitality (emotional life, aesthetic sensibility, pleasures), agency (sense of mastery and empowerment, social recognition), belonging (network, social capital) and meaning (continuity of tradition, transcendental values, hope). Cohen *et al.* (2006) found that older people with mood disorders who engaged in choral participation, in contrast with a comparison group who undertook different activities, reported improved general health and morale, reduced loneliness, had fewer visits to doctors and reported a reduction in the number of over-the-counter medications taken.

Following the general community music imperative, and in order to explore the viability of singing programmes for older people in the Australian context, a project was started in 2007, with funding from the regional arts and health sponsors Healthway, Silver Chain (a home care service provider for the elderly) and seed funding from the University of Western Australia.

The study used community musicians to conduct the singing groups. The intention was to investigate improvements in the wellbeing of older people participating in singing groups. The studies undertaken sought to identify factors that may have facilitated any improvements and contributed to the group experience.

The study involved an examination of six community choirs involving choristers all over 70 years of age. Some of the choirs involved in this study included dementia patients and their carers. Both qualitative and quantitative analyses were conducted in order to investigate the following questions:

i   In what ways can community singing facilitate grieving by the elderly and dementia sufferers?
ii In what ways can participation in community singing assist carers to prepare for the future loss of the cared-for individual?
iii In what ways can involvement in the singing groups help the elderly and their carers to celebrate life and the time they have left together?

---

1 http://www.soundsense.org

Embracing Life in the Face of Death   117

Given the demographics of the participants, the singers involved were typically experiencing several of the above-mentioned types of grief: grief over the loss of spouses and other loved ones, grief over the loss of autonomy and previous ways of life, preparatory grief over one's own mortality; and anticipatory grief experienced by caregivers over the inevitable future loss of the one they care for. It was hoped that the singing groups would both facilitate the grieving processes the participants were likely to be experiencing, and would result in giving them opportunities to celebrate the lives they had led in the past and connections they could continue to enjoy in the future.

Research Design and Method

Participants

Longitudinally, the work involved the formation of six singing groups, each comprising a membership of 18–75 people, the vast majority of whom were over 70 years of age, and all based in the Perth Metro area of Western Australia (see Table 10.1). A total of 234 choristers have been members of these choirs, though membership has ebbed and flowed as people have moved on (a euphemism here for those who have literally changed homes and those who have sadly died).

It took a period of 16 months to devise the programme and set up the groups, using physical and mental exercises based on vocal and physical warm-ups and songs selected for the cohorts based on pilot work and knowledge of other such groups across the world. The membership comprised those seeking a new activity, and although singing was the known focus of the activity, many people were initially highly reluctant to engage with the activity, feeling that they were too old, or had never shown skill or had the opportunity to try singing as an experience. The explicit aims of the groups were to provide regular opportunities to practise and develop a range of participants' musical/singing skills alongside social, cognitive, emotional and physical skills reported to be associated with the experience of singing. All groups are referred to by acronyms to protect the identity of individuals: SSS, PWC, RoL and HH were all seniors groups

Table 10.1 Group participants

Group	Number at inception	Mean age (in years)	Gender split Women: Men
SSS	36	81	3:1
PWC	28	60+	3:1
RoL	75	61	4:1
HH	22	74–	2:1
MZ	28	40+ (range 42–102)	3:1
FiH	18	34+ (range 34–86)	3:1

118   *Jane W. Davidson*

developed out of centres for seniors (such as the City of Mandurah), or were run out of local council facilities (the City of Stirling choir). Two groups of choristers involved people living with mild dementia and their carers, MZ and FiH. A summary table of participants is shown in Table 10.1. Please note that the carers were obviously of a younger age range, hence the age ranges of membership are also shown. With 36 x 2 hour workshops per year for each group, the project has offered longitudinal opportunity to develop the potential for answers to the questions posed above.

Data Collection

Over the seven-year period of the programme, and its roll out (note that singing groups were begun in a staggered manner) intermittent questionnaires, face-to-face interviews and group discussions have taken place to sample experience. The majority of the surveys were conducted during the group sessions, but some were conducted by being sent home with participants to be returned at a later meeting in order to minimise interruption to the singing group activities. Some of these data are reported elsewhere (Davidson & Faulkner, 2010; Davidson & Fedele, 2011; Davidson, 2011; Davidson *et al.*, in press; Sataloff and Davidson, 2012).

The instruments used for data collection included the short version of the World Health Organization Quality of Life Assessment (WHOQOL-BREF); the SF-36v2 Health Survey; the UCLA Loneliness Scale (Russell, 1996); the Geriatric Depression Scale (GDS, Yesavage *et al.*, 1983); the Hierarchic Dementia Scale (HDS, Cole & Dastoor, 1987); the Quality of Life – Alzheimer's Disease (QoL-AD, Logsdon *et al.*, 2002); and some general questions about musical activities, expectations and outcomes. In addition, caregivers provided ratings on mood, energy, concentration and stress levels at weeks two, four and six, both pre- and post-session.

For this specific chapter, a summary of pertinent quantitative data is provided along with qualitative reports from a handful of participants. These comments are indicative, often reflecting the views of many more participants.

Data Analysis

Thematic analysis was used for examination of the narratives collected during the interviews (Braun & Clarke, 2006). Given the scope of this project, not all the measures and questionnaires used were expected to yield data relevant to this study. Therefore, the qualitative data which was relevant to the questions being investigated in this study were categorised according to codes chosen based on the literature discussed above and the expected influences of the singing programmes on the participants (Sobh & Perry, 2006). Once the data had been sorted according to these codes, the patterns were analysed and combined to create themes and sub-themes. Initially the data were coded under the following topics: social connection, mood and expression of grief.

Table 10.2 Dominant themes from the data

Social Connection	Mood	Expression and Validation of Grief	Life Review	Physical Rejuvenation	Renewed interest in Life
Loneliness reduced	Mood scores improved	Communication of emotions without words	Reflecting on the past	Physical benefits of breathing exercises	Renewal of generalised hope
Group cooperation on tasks	Relaxation levels increased	Sense of understanding each other	Sharing memories with carer	Increased energy and vitality levels	Opportunities to learn new skills
Sharing of experience and emotions		Sense of understanding from the music	Imbuing past experiences with worth		Thrill of performance
Group cohesion and friendship					

Results and Discussion

Several themes were noted in analysing the data. The primary themes that emerged from the data were: social connection, expression and validation of grief, life review, mood improvement, physical rejuvenation, and renewed interest in life (see Table 10.2). These themes will be discussed individually below.

Social Connection

Whilst a relationship between ageing and social isolation, low social support, depression, and other chronic health problems has been reported (Bunker, Colquhoun & Murrary, 2003; Sorkin, Rook & Lu, 2002), meaningful social engagement is described as one pathway by which the wellbeing of older people might be enhanced (Greaves & Farbus, 2006). One particular benefit of participation in group singing is the opportunity for social connection. Such social support has been consistently shown to mitigate the stress of grief (Duke, 1998). Social interaction assists the elderly to tolerate the pain of loss and achieve a sense of completion in relationships (MacKenzie, 2011).

There is good evidence to show the positive social effect of singing in groups. In the current study, participants had the opportunity to meet with and work alongside new people. Singing together also provided opportunities to enhance relationships between caregivers and the cared-for. This was built on the group activities in the current study that included cooperating together in warm-ups or small-group singing, and also choosing songs.

120   *Jane W. Davidson*

The FiH and MZ caregivers had improved scores on the 'social relationship' domain of the WHOQOL-BREF and there was a reduction in scores on the UCLA Loneliness Scale, although not at a statistically significant level (p = .08). For the SSS group, scores on the UCLA Loneliness Scale revealed a gradual reduction from time one to time four (slope of the linear regression was negative: −803). For the others, there was no change.

> I catch glimpses of how he used to be when he sings. It is a good change for me too.

> It is none of those scary things I thought it could be. I've made a new network of people.

Singing together also helped people to feel connected via a sense of group cohesion and the immediacy of emotions shared in the music. Participants reported feeling a strong sense of friendship, even intimacy with their fellow singers.

> Sometimes I just sit there and think: this music is helping us all to be together. It puts you into the same space and on the same wave-length. Gets you into the here and now.

> We do call and response songs sort of 'heigh-ho' (call)/'heigh-ho' (response) and Gladys just loves it, with her sort of dementia, she can't really catch onto a lot of what's going on in the world around her, but that sort of exercise seems to stimulate her and let her get involved.

> Being in a group and singing is a deeply physical and emotional experience. I can feel the hairs rise on the back of my neck as I feel the vibrations of the low male bass voices singing behind me. When people get older, they don't experience physical contact the way they used to when they were young. When I sing, I can literally feel the caress of the breath of others close to me; I can feel us all breathing together, being close and intimate in the harmonies.

Expression and Validation of Grief

Singing can also enable expression of emotions around loss and grief which patients have not otherwise been able to express (Magee & Davidson, 2004). Aldridge (1999), for example, describes how singing with a dying friend heightened understanding where words were potentially awkward, or inadequate. Singing is something that nearly everyone can participate in, having a low threshold for involvement. In fact studies show that even when language skills have deteriorated, dementia patients may still be capable of singing (Cuddy, 2005; Prickett & Moore, 1991). At times, the music itself seems to offer understanding.

> Without words we can understand one another in the music.

> Sometimes you just understand your neighbour through the tone of their voice and the look they give you.

Embracing Life in the Face of Death 121

Our members living with dementia certainly understand the group atmosphere, the sensitivity of the music (sometimes they laugh, sometimes they cry – often very appropriately) the melody, the harmonies.

Life Review

Another important way in which participation in group music-making can facilitate grieving is by helping the elderly to make sense of their lives and to imbue past events with meaning and worth. Reflecting on their past, both the great moments and the disappointments, is an important part of preparatory grieving. Magee and Davidson (2004) describe the use of singing activities with individuals in the late stages of multiple sclerosis to permit the use of songs for reminiscence value. Familiar song repertoire, in particular, has been shown to be useful in one-to-one therapeutic contexts for life review in palliative care (Aldridge, 1999). Group musicking could be a valuable opportunity for sufferers of both preparatory and anticipatory grief to gather memories of events experienced with their loved ones as well as to explore and reflect upon memories in a safe and structured environment. Indeed, part of the training and developing of the programme with the facilitators was around selecting repertoire and then getting the membership to select and introduce new songs.

> I wouldn't say I got teary, but when you haven't heard those songs for so many years and your memory goes back . . . to when you sort of . . . family company and that.

> I used the tune from 'Tea for Two' and wrote about 'me and you!', talking about when me and my old man met.

> That song called 'Why we sing' stirs you up and gets your heart pounding. The melody and the harmony – all of it – just gets you going. I love that song. It is our choir's anthem. It is emotional and music is like that. That's why I love singing.

Mood Improvement

Various studies also indicate that mood improvement can be an additional benefit of engaging in group musical activities. MacKenzie (2011) recommends music therapy among other things for calming anxiety. Clift *et al.*'s (2009) study of over 600 choristers revealed benefits for psychological wellbeing, including effects on mood.

In the current study, the caregivers from the FiH and MZ groups had improved scores on the psychological health domain of the WHOQOL-BREF. There was also no indication of depression on the GDS following involvement in the singing group sessions. Mood was significantly improved on the post-test scores $t(9) = -3.000$, $p < .05$. A significant benefit from attending consecutive sessions was observed in the caregivers' level of Relaxation $F(1, 4) = 8.955$, $p < .05$. The RoL group also demonstrated significant improvements from pre- to post- singing group sessions in Mood $t(29) = -2.728$, $p < .05$, and Relaxation $t(29) = 2.715$, $p < .05$.

122   *Jane W. Davidson*

Before I did the singing group I used to get stuck in my mood and in one of those times. Singing helps to see that life isn't so bad.

Physical Rejuvenation

Evidence suggests that singing can also be physically rejuvenating for participants (Magee & Davidson, 2004). Indeed, Cohen *et al.* (2006) found that those who attended singing groups were far more energised and incurred fewer trips to the doctors than their colleagues in other activity or control groups.

The FiH and MZ caregivers demonstrated significant improvements on the Vitality health domain of the SF37v2 survey (p < .01). Energy was also significantly improved $t(9) = -3.000$, p < .05). The RoL group similarly experienced improvements in Energy $t(29) = -3.958$, p < .001.

Warm-ups make you aware of your body, and that helps you feel alive: sensing every bit of yourself. Sometimes we dance and stuff and that is real fun. Singing and dancing is what it is about: getting yourself in contact with your life, and energy! It makes you feel better, uplifted, fitter and healthier.

Renewed Interest in Life

As people age, they tend not to have opportunities to learn new skills, yet research shows that the challenge of new skills helps people to feel able and valued. Attendance at the singing groups provided opportunities for participants to develop new skills. Performing added considerably to the experience. Participants gained a sense of pride in the achievement and increased feelings of self-worth and being valued by others. The renewed sense of hope enabled participants to have a reinvigorated interest in life and to further value relationships with others (Mystakidou *et al.*, 2009).

I used to sing all the time as a child: in the playground, with my Mum at the park. But that is different to being in a proper choir. I mean, being at home isn't really proper singing – you know, being able to sing scales, harmonies, hold a line . . . It is a great new challenge.

You reflect on life and you think: 'Why not give it a go, you've got nothing else to lose!' When you sing with the others there is a discipline to it. I didn't realise how precise it has to be: come in together; blend in together; pronounce your words clearly; try to sing that high note stronger or softer; watch your tuning. There's a precision and beauty to it. Being a singer is not easy, but it is better and more enjoyable that I imagined. Being a singer also means you've got to be a team player. Team-building can be challenging [*smirks*].

Something inside me said: 'Have a go, because if you don't do it now, you'll never do it.' So, I did, and I've never regretted it for a second. I plucked up the courage to go and I did it.

Embracing Life in the Face of Death 123

My grandchildren thought it was brilliant that I was going to be performing in a concert. Of course I go and see them at swimming events and in school concerts, but when all the family came to see and hear me in a concert, now that was something special! I've never been one for the spotlight. Getting applause and being praised in public is important recognition. It gives you worth. I don't think I've ever had applause for anything else I do.

When you get up in a concert and all those eyes are looking at you, then applauding you and praising you; well it is fabulous.

Performing gives another side to my sense of who I am. I feel good at what I'm doing. I'm no trained musician, but I can do the job and other people tell me that.

Conclusions

Socially isolated elderly persons, as well as elderly persons living with dementia, were engaged in healthy social participation through group singing activities and events. Many of these people expressed their joy and love for the singing group and the individuals involved, confirming the favourable benefits to their mental health. The group singing programmes provided opportunities for elderly persons with dementia to participate in singing together with their caregivers. Caregivers in particular from both these groups have reported pleasure at seeing their partner with dementia engaged in and enjoying the singing activities, and at having the opportunity to participate in an activity together. In addition to these notable relational benefits, participants with more advanced stages of dementia in some groups have been observed to 'come out of their shell' and interact more with their caregiver and the people around them during singing activities.

The benefits appeared to be particularly great for the caregivers following their involvement in the singing group sessions. Reports from the caregivers revealed that they thoroughly enjoyed being part of the singing group, partly to observe the positive impacts experienced by their partners with dementia, but also to provide a social context for them to relax, and to engage in a physically and mentally stimulating activity.

Our work has demonstrated that regular involvement in singing group sessions results in a variety of improvements, for instance, caregivers of persons with dementia have improved vitality, on the SF36v2, as well as increased energy levels, and an improved mood. Further singing group members that regularly attended the singing sessions demonstrated a positive follow on effect that was evident in attendance at the next singing session.

Interestingly, whilst the carers gained significant positive benefit from singing in the dementia-focused groups, members of RoL who were non-dementia and all living independent lives as seniors also seemed to gain much benefit. Two clarifications are required here, however. Firstly, RoL was a younger membership than the other non-dementia groups and generally had fewer health complaints than the

124 *Jane W. Davidson*

older groups such as SSS, HH or PWC, who did not seem to show many quantitative changes in their health, though their qualitative reports offered rich insights.

In addition, the choice of songs that had personal relevance to the participants enabled them to reflect on their lives and to share memories with others in the group and with their carers. This is an important part of the grieving process for both those experiencing preparatory grief and those experiencing grief in anticipation of the loss of a loved one. Furthermore, the improved sense of general wellbeing and mood along with the increased opportunities to enjoy social interaction was able to give some participants a renewed interest in life. The overall improvements led to a sense of renewed hope in a generalised sense even where specific hopes had failed. Opportunities to develop new skills were a surprising source of pleasure for participants, giving them a sense that there were still things to be enjoyed in their remaining years of life, despite increasing infirmity and loss of previous lifestyles.

Therefore, our research findings promote singing involvement as a method to improve mental health and wellbeing outcomes for the singing group members, and to provide a context for healthy social interaction. These benefits may be of particular value to the elderly, dementia patients and their carers in facilitating their grief and giving them opportunities to gather new memories, thus stimulating their interest in embracing life. Further, promoting regular attendance at singing groups is recommended given the additional benefit gained from such consistency.

References

Aldridge, D. (1999). *Music Therapy in Palliative Care: New Voices*. London: Jessica Kingsley Publishers.

Braun, V., & Clarke, V. (2006). Using thematic analysis in psychology. *Qualitative Research in Psychology, 3*, 77–101.

Bunker, S., Colquhoun, D., & Murrary, D. (2003). Stress and coronary heart disease: Psychosocial risk factors, National Heart Foundation position statement update. *Medical Journal of Australia, 178*, 272–276.

Clift, S., Hancox, G., Morrison, I., Hess, B., Kreutz, G., & Stewart, D. (2009). Choral singing and psychological wellbeing: Quantitative and qualitative findings from English choirs in a cross-national survey. *Journal of Applied Arts and Health, 1*, 19–34.

Cohen, G. D., Perlstein, S., Chapline, J., Kelly, J., Firth, K. M., & Simmens, S. (2006). The impact of professionally conducted cultural programs on the physical health, mental health, and social functioning of older adults. *The Gerontologist, 46*, 726–734.

Cole, M. G., & Dastoor, D. P. (1987). The course of multi-infarct dementia: An uncontrolled longitudinal study. *Journal of Clinical and Experimental Gerontology, 10*, 13–22.

Collins, C., Liken, S., King, S., & Kokinakis, C. (1993). Loss and grief among dementia caregivers. *Qualitative Health Research, 3*, 236–253.

Cuddy, L. A. (2005). Music, memory, and Alzheimer's disease: is music recognition spared in dementia and how can it be assessed? *Medical Hypothesis, 64*, 229–235.

Davidson, J. W., & Fedele, J. (2011). Investigating group singing activity with people with dementia and their caregivers: Problems and positive prospects. *Musicae Scientiae, 15*, 402–422.

Embracing Life in the Face of Death 125

Duke, S. (1998). An exploration of anticipatory grief: the lived experience of people during their spouses' terminal illness and in bereavement. *Journal of Advanced Nursing, 28*, 829–839.

Gerber, I., Rusalem, R., Hannon, N., Battin, D., & Arkin, A. (1975). Anticipatory grief and aged widows and widowers. *Journal of Gerontology, 30*, 225–229.

Gilliland, G., & Fleming, S. (1998). A comparison of spousal anticipatory grief and conventional grief. *Death Studies, 22*, 541–569.

Greaves, C. J., & Farbus, L. (2006). Effects of creative and social activity on the health and well-being of socially isolated people: Outcomes from a multi-method observational study. *The Journal of the Royal Society for the Promotion of Health, 126*, 134–142.

Humphrey, G. M., & Kimpfer, D. G. (2008). *Counselling for Grief and Bereavement* (2nd ed.). London: SAGE Publications Ltd.

Kubler-Ross, E. (1969). *On Death and Dying*: Routledge.

Lee, C. (1996). *Music at the Edge: The Music Therapy Experiences of a Musician with AIDS*. London & New York: Routledge.

Lindemann, E. (1944). Symptomatology and management of acute grief. *American Journal of Psychiatry, 101*, 141–148.

Lindgren, C. L., Connelly, C. T., & Gaspar, H. L. (1999). Grief in spouse and children caregivers of dementia patients. *Western Journal of Nursing Research, 21*, 521–537.

Logsdon, R. G., Gibbons, L. E., McCurry, S. M., & Teri, L. (2002). Assessing quality of life in older adults with cognitive impairment. *Psychosomatic Medicine, 64*, 510–519.

MacKenzie, M. A. (2011). Preparatory grief in frail elderly individuals. *Annals of Long-Term Care: Clinical Care and Aging, 19*, 22–56.

Magee, W. L., & Davidson, J. W. (2004). Music therapy in Multiple Sclerosis: Results of a systematic qualitative analysis. *Music Therapy Perspectives, 22*, 39–51.

Mystakidou, K., Parpa, E., Tsilika, E., Athanasouli, P., Pathiaku, M., Galanos, A., *et al.* (2008). Preparatory grief, psychological distress and hopelessness in advanced cancer patients. *European Journal of Cancer Care, 17*, 145–151.

Mystakidou, K., Tsilika, E., Parpa, E., Athanasouli, P., Galanos, A., Pagoropoulou, A., *et al.* (2009). Illness-related hopelessness in advanced cancer: Influence of anxiety, depression and preparatory grief. *Archives of Psychiatric Nursing, 23*, 138–147.

Oxford English Dictionary (2012). Oxford: Oxford University Press.

Parkes, M. C. (1998). Bereavement in adult life. *British Medical Journal, 316*, 856–859.

Periyakoil, V. S., & Hallenbeck, J. (2002). Identifying and managing preparatory grief and depression at the end of life. *American Family Physician, 65*, 883–891.

Prickett, C. A., & Moore, R. S. (1991). The use of music to aid memory of Alzheimer's patients. *Journal of Music Therapy, 28*, 101–110.

Rando, T. A. (1986). *Loss, Anticipatroy Grief*. Lexington, MA: Lexington Books.

Russell, D. (1996). The UCLA Loneliness Scale (Version 3): Reliability, validity, and factor structure. *Journal of Personality Assessment, 66*, 20–40.

Ruud, E. (2012). The new health musicians. In R. MacDonald, G. Kreutz & L. Mitchell (Eds.), *Music, Health, & Wellbeing*. Oxford: Oxford University Press.

Sanders, C. M. (1982). Effects of sudden vs. chronic illness death on bereavement outcome. *Omega, 13*, 227–232.

Small, C. (1998). *Musicking: The Meanings of Performing and Listening*. Hanover, NH: Wesleyan University Press.

Sobh, R., & Perry, C. (2006). Research design and data analysis in realism research. *European Journal of Marketing, 40*, 1,194–1,209.

Sorkin, D., Rook, K. S., & Lu, J. L. (2002). Loneliness, lack of emotional support, lack of companionship, and the likelihood of having a heart condition in an elderly sample. *Annals of Behavioural Medicine, 24*, 290–298.

Stige, B., Ansdell, G., & Elefant, C. (2010). Where Music Helps: Community Music Therapy in Action and Reflection. Surrey: Gower Publishing Ltd.

Yesavage, J. A., Brink, T. L., Rose, T. L., Lum, O., Huang, V., Adey, M. B., *et al.* (1983). Development and validation of a geriatric depression screening scale: A preliminary report. Journal of Psychiatric Research, 17, 37–49.

Index

Aasgaard, T. 97–98
Aboriginal Australians 4, 83–96
acoustic communities 33
Adamson, S. 12, 26
ADC websites 41–42
adjustment after loss 27, 64
aesthetics 22–28
Afro-American funerals 56;
    see also jazz funerals
after death communications (ADCs)
    41–43
age 23, 24
agula spirits 86
Aldridge, D. 115, 120
Ali, Imam 71
alteration 53
Anderson, M.J. 64
angel of history 81
anguma spirits 86, 87, 94
anticipatory grief 4, 27, 115, 117,
    121, 124
Armstrong, L. 73, 81
arousal 22–27
Attali, J. 31–32
Australia 1; Aboriginal communities 4,
    83–96
autonomy, loss of 114–115, 117

baby-boom generation 79–82
Barria, J. 59
Barthes, R. 50, 51
Barwick, L. 92
Beeman, W.O. 74
bell tolling 3, 31–39
Benjamin, W. 73, 81
bereavement support group 4, 101–110

'Binnorie' ('The Twa Sisters') 44–46, 53
birth 87, 88
Booth, General B. 11
Bordemar 59
Bourne, H. 31
Bright, R. 98
Bronson, B.H. 52
burrunguma spirits 86, 90, 91

Calvin, J. 9
'cantos de ángeles' 3–4, 57–65
caregivers 115; community singing
    groups including 116–124
Castle, J. 2, 65
celebration: funeral music choices 14–16,
    24, 27; psychological function of music
    in mourning rituals 56, 61–62
challenges 108
Chamberlain, J. 35–36
Chidley, S. 33
child funerals 57–59
Chilean 'cantos de ángeles' 3–4, 57–65
choral settings 5–6, 7
Christian funeral music 9–10
Christian pop music 26–27
Claes, M. 22
classical music 20–27
Clift, S. 121
Cohen, G.D. 116, 122
co-inherence 87–88, 90, 92–93
Collins, S. 46, 47, 53
community singing groups 4, 115–124
confidentiality 108
conscientiousness 23, 24, 25
containment 88–89
Cook, G. 59

128 *Index*

Co-operative Funeralcare 11
coping: strategies 60; styles 21–22, 23,
    24–27; young people and music therapy
    102–103, 109
Country 86, 87, 88, 94
Courts, C. 37
Crawford, E. 10
crematoriums 10
Cressy, D. 31, 33, 34, 36
'Cruel Mother, The' 46–47, 51, 52–53

Dagenham cobbler 36–38
dancing 84, 89–94
Davidson, J.W. 121
Deghati, S. 79, 80
dementia, people with 115, 116–124
DeNora, T. 98
Devers, E. 42–43
Diana, Princess of Wales 2, 59
distributed identities 87–88
drum improvisation 106–107
Dulugun 86, 90

ecological models of bereavement
    100–101
ecologically informed research 101–110
Eerola, T. 20
elderly people 27, 114–126; community
    singing groups 4, 115–124
elegiac singing 4, 69–82
Elizabeth I 35
Ellison, R. 73
Emke, I. 59
emotion-focused coping 60
emotional communities 31–33
emotional content 14–15
emotional space 109
emotions 98–99, 103, 110
empty chair tecÛique 98
England 3, 31–39
entertainment 74
Essex cobbler 36–38
everyday performance genre 4, 83–96
expression of grief 62–63, 118, 119,
    120–121

Facebook 77, 78–79
Feld, S. 55
festivals 89

Floyd, A.E. 10
Freud, S. 40, 41, 43, 47–49, 50
friendly ghosts 41–43
fun 107
funeral marches 10
funeral music choices 2–3, 9–30;
    explorative study 13–16; large-scale
    survey 18, 21–28; pilot study 19–21
funerals 1, 2; modern secular 59–65; Pip
    Maddern's funeral 5–7; psychological
    function of music 3–4, 55–68;
    secularisation of 1, 16, 59

Garrido, S. 21–22
Garrioch, D. 33
geno-song 51
genotext 50, 51, 52
genre classification 19–20
genre clusters 20, 22–23
Georgian laments 3, 57, 59–65
ghosts 3, 40–54; friendly and vengeful
    41–43
globalisation 1–2
Goss, R. 65–66
grief 2; anticipatory 4, 27, 115, 117, 121,
    124; expression of 62–63, 118, 119,
    120–121; preparatory 4, 114, 117, 121,
    124; shared grieving 62–63; types of
    114–115; validation of 119,
    120–121
grief resolution 55
Grimby, A. 40
Grocke, D. 98
Guarda, S. 59

Hartley, N. 98
haunting music 3, 40–54
Hayden, B. 1
Helali, A.R. 70, 71–72, 74–79, 80
Helle, A. 43
heya'ati ('group members'
    in Tehran) 74
Hirsch, M. 79–80
Holloway, M. 12, 26, 61
Homer 1
horror films 43
Hossein, Imam 70–71, 73, 74
Hosseiniah, the 70–73, 80
Howard, H. 34–36, 38

Index 129

humorous music 20–27
hymns 6–7, 9

ihram 79
impending death 27, 97–98, 114–126;
    community singing groups 4, 115–124
improvisation 98, 106–107
incantation 53
incremental repetition 53
independence, loss of 114–115, 117
'Indian hawkers' 10–11
infanticide 46–47
instrumental music 10, 20–27
Inti-Illimani 59
intimacy 120
Iran 4, 69–82
Iran–Iraq war 69, 73, 74–75, 79,
    80–81
Islamic cool 70, 76, 78–79
isorhythmic performance 93

Jadmi-style Junba 90
James I and VI 35
jazz funerals 3, 56–57, 59–65
Jerregorl-style Junba 91
Josselin, R. 37–38
'Judas' 43
Junba 85, 89–94
juxtaposition 92–93

Karbala 70, 73, 74
Kastenbaum, R. 59
Keen, K. 41
Khomeini, Ayatollah 79, 81
Klass, D. 55, 61, 65–66
Kleinpaul, R. 43
Kotthoff, H. 62
Kristeva, J. 50–51, 52
Kubler-Ross, E. 2

Lacan, J. 50–51
lalangue 50–51, 52
laments 3, 57, 59–65
Lancashire, England 34
LaRue, C. 44, 45
Lee, C. 98, 115
Levitin, D. 116
life review 119, 121, 124
Lindemann, E. 115

linguistic theory 50–51
Luther, M. 9

MacKenzie, M.A. 121
Maddahs (professional mourners)
    69–70, 72–73, 73–74; Helali 70,
    71–72, 74–79, 80
Maddern, P. 4–8; funeral 5–7; memorial
    service 7
Magee, W.L. 121
Magowan, F. 83
Mahdi, Imam 71
Marett, A. 83
Martin, M.D. 92
Martin, S.N. 91
martyrs 71, 74, 80
McFerran, K.S. 100
melancholia 48–49
melodic setting of texts 93
memorial service 7
memory 73; remembering the
    good things 103
merging of voices 92
Miranda, D. 22
Moha (Helali) 75–76
Moharram 1384 (Helali) 75
mood creation 14–16, 18–28
mood improvement 118, 119, 121–122
moving forward 103–104
Moyle, A. 83–84
Mozart's Requiem 22, 23, 24
murder 43–49
music choices for funerals *see* funeral
    music choices
music therapy: for adolescents 4, 97–113;
    community singing 4, 115–124; in
    palliative care 97–98, 121
music videos 70, 71–72
musical relationship 106–107
musicianship 107
My Life As a Playlist website 18, 22

narratives, personal 63
neurotic patients 48, 49
neuroticism 23, 25, 27
Never Weather-beaten Sail (Campion) 5
New Orleans jazz funerals 3, 56–57, 59–65
Ngarinyin communities 84, 85–93
nohe khani (elegiac singing) 4, 69–82

130 *Index*

noise 31–32
northern Australia 4, 83–96
nostalgia 21–22, 23, 25

O sacrum convivium (Tallis) 6
O'Callaghan, C. 61, 97
O'Grady, L. 100
ongoing connection with the deceased 61
organ music 7

palliative care 27; music therapy
    97–98, 121
Panzera, C. 51
parishes 32–33
Parra, V. 58, 59
performance genres 4, 83–96
personal meaning/expression
    12, 14–16, 18–28
personal narratives 63
personality factors 21–27
personhood 85–89
pheno-song 51
phenotext 50, 52
Philips, W.L. 2, 65
physical memorials 61
physical rejuvenation 119, 122
Pilkington, J. 34
place 109
plague 37–38
poetic tecÛiques 92–93
popular music 72; funeral music choices
    11, 20–27; Iran 80–81
postmemory 79–82
pre-death (anticipatory) grief 4, 27, 115,
    117, 121, 124
preparatory grief 4, 114, 117, 121, 124
primitive societies 48, 49
privacy 108
problem-focused coping 60
progressive incorporation 87
Protestantism 33–34
psalms 6, 7
psychological function of music 3–4, 55–68
purgatory, elimination of 33

quality of life 116

Radsdale, G. 37
Ram, M. 10–11

recorded (relayed) music 10
Redmond, A. 84, 85, 87–88, 90, 91, 94
Reformation 32, 33–34
relayed music 10
religious conviction 64–65
renewed interest in life 119, 122–123, 124
repetition 52–53
requiems 9; Mozart's Requiem 22, 23, 24
re-ritualisation 2, 59
resilience 100
restoration 85, 87–89; Junba 89–94
revenant ballads 3, 40–41, 43–53
rhythmic setting 93
rituals 1, 2; psychological function of
    music 3–4, 55–68; re-ritualisation 2, 59
Roberts, M. 100
Robinson, K.M. 42
Roman Catholicism 34–36, 38
Rosenwein, R. 31–32
Ross, M.C. 83
Ruud, E. 116

Saari, P. 20
sacred/traditional music 20–27
sacredness, atmosphere of 64–65
Saeedi, S. 72
Saynor, J.K. 2
Schechter, J.M. 62, 64
Scher, I.L. 46
Schubert, E. 21–22
secular funerals 59–65
secular music 11
secularisation of funerals 1, 16, 59
Secundy, M.G. 63
self-expression 105, 106
self-reproach 48–49
sequential exploratory design 13
shared grieving 62–63
Shia Islam 69
shifting affiliations 79–82
Si bona suscepimus (de Lassus) 6
Sicut cervus (Palestrina) 7
Silverman, P.R. 55, 61
singing *see* songs and singing
Skewes, K. 100
small group music therapy 108
social connection 14–15; music therapy
    104, 110, 118, 119–120; psychological
    function of music 62–63

Index   131

social support 104–105, 110
songs and singing 98; community singing
    groups 4, 115–124; conception of Junba
    dance-songs 90; elegiac singing 4,
    69–82; functions of song 116; music
    therapy 4, 98, 105–106, 115–124;
    northern Australian Aboriginals 84–85,
    89–94; revenant ballads as song 49–53;
    writing 98, 105–106
Sound Sense 116
space, emotional 109
Spain 58
spirits: haunting music 3, 40–54;
    Ngarinyin communities 86, 87,
    88, 90, 91, 94
Sufi trance music 80–81

tags 19–20
task-based coping 60
teenagers *see* young people
terminal illness 27, 114; *see also*
    impending death, palliative care
texts of Junba songs 91–93
thematic analysis 14
Thou knowest Lord (Purcell) 7
tolling of bells 3, 31–39
tormenting scruples 48–49
tradition 12, 14–15, 18–28
traditional/sacred music 20–27

transcorporealisation 87
TRU paranormal website 42
Truax, B. 33
'Twa Sisters, The' ('Binnorie') 44–46, 53

United States (US) 1; jazz funerals 3,
    56–57, 59–65

valence 19, 20, 22–27
validation of grief 119, 120–121
vengeful dead 43

Walter, T. 59
wanjina spirits 86, 87, 88, 94
war martyrs 71, 74, 80
Weber, J. 10
wellbeing: bereavement support music
    therapy for adolescents 102–105;
    community singing groups
    and 116–124
Westermarck, E.A. 47–48
Wild, S. 83
wisdom-of-spirit.com 49–50
Wouters, C. 26
wunggurr spirits 86

young people 4, 97–113; music, emotions
    and 98–99; music therapy bereavement
    support group 4, 101–110

eBooks
from Taylor & Francis

Helping you to choose the right eBooks for your Library

Add to your library's digital collection today with Taylor & Francis eBooks. We have over 50,000 eBooks in the Humanities, Social Sciences, Behavioural Sciences, Built Environment and Law, from leading imprints, including Routledge, Focal Press and Psychology Press.

Choose from a range of subject packages or create your own!

Benefits for you
- Free MARC records
- COUNTER-compliant usage statistics
- Flexible purchase and pricing options
- All titles DRM-free.

Benefits for your user
- Off-site, anytime access via Athens or referring URL
- Print or copy pages or chapters
- Full content search
- Bookmark, highlight and annotate text
- Access to thousands of pages of quality research at the click of a button.

Free Trials Available
We offer free trials to qualifying academic, corporate and government customers.

eCollections

Choose from over 30 subject eCollections, including:

Archaeology	Language Learning
Architecture	Law
Asian Studies	Literature
Business & Management	Media & Communication
Classical Studies	Middle East Studies
Construction	Music
Creative & Media Arts	Philosophy
Criminology & Criminal Justice	Planning
Economics	Politics
Education	Psychology & Mental Health
Energy	Religion
Engineering	Security
English Language & Linguistics	Social Work
Environment & Sustainability	Sociology
Geography	Sport
Health Studies	Theatre & Performance
History	Tourism, Hospitality & Events

For more information, pricing enquiries or to order a free trial, please contact your local sales team:
www.tandfebooks.com/page/sales

www.tandfebooks.com